Profitable Herb-Growing
at Home

PROFITABLE
HERB-GROWING
AT HOME

Betty E. M. Jacobs

Illustrations by Charles H. Joslin

Garden Way Publishing
Charlotte, Vermont 05445

Printed in the United States by Essex Publishing Company

Designed by David Robinson

Cover design by Braren/Trezzo Studio

Also by the same author:

Growing Herbs for the Kitchen, published by Gray's Publishing Ltd., Sidney, B.C., Canada

Library of Congress Cataloging in Publication Data

Jacobs, Betty E M
    Profitable herb-growing at home.

    Bibliography: p.
    Includes index.
    1. Herb gardening. I. Title.
SB351.H5J32   635'.7   74-12665
ISBN 0-88266-087-X

Contents

Dr. Johnson: "Give me the town, Sir. The Countryman may be king of his holdings, yet, I tell you, Sir, he is the slave of his own acres."

Squire Windrum: "Yes, Sir. But where will you find such willing servitude, or such happy kingship?"

Preface

My husband and I had often talked of writing a book on growing Herbs for profit, but until we retired from growing Herbs commercially, we couldn't find the time. We hope this book will be of help to all who want to make a profit from Herb growing—both those who are just starting and others who have already established their Herb gardens.

Our experience—starting and running a Herb farm for eight years on southern Vancouver Island, in Canada, a lifetime interest in Herbs, and the success of our first book, *Growing Herbs for the Kitchen*—gives us a unique background to help others get started in a field that is uncrowded and has great potential. Herb growing *can* be profitable, but you must start small and grow with your markets.

This is a book for people of all ages who want to turn over a modest profit from their Herbs and then gradually expand into a business that need be limited only by the time they have to devote to it and their own ingenuity. Profits do not depend on the amount of land available.

Few people today can go out and buy the "ideal" place to start a Herb farm or nursery. Even if they could afford such a place, it would be hard to find. So let us assume that you have a house and some land available, and that you are willing to adapt yourself within the limits that house and land impose.

You must not expect to make enough money to live on during the first eighteen months or two years after planting a new Herb garden. So, unless you have some other source of income, one of you (I am assuming that two people are working together in this) will have to go on with an outside job till both your garden and your markets are well established.

The term *Herbs* covers many different plants from several botanical families, and no matter what people tell you, Herbs are not "just weeds." They need as much care in cultivation as any other garden plants. So a basic knowledge of gardening is essential, and some knowledge of Herbs and their growing needs is a help.

There are many different ways to sell the Herbs you grow; no matter what your skills and interests are, they can all be used in one way or another. You may wish to raise fresh culinary Herbs for restaurants, to dry Herbs for the culinary and medicinal market, to make Catnip toys for pet shops, or even to start a line of gourmet salad dressings—whatever your choice, you will have plenty of uses for the Herbs you grow.

What you need are the raw materials from plants, so let's get on with the soil preparation and planting so that you can start growing Herbs for profit.

BETTY E. M. JACOBS

To T. J.

ANGELICA (*Angelica archangelica*)

CHAPTER 1

To Help You Get Started

Whatever land you have available to start your Herb-growing operations, your main objective will be to make the most profitable use of it. There will be a number of things which will have to be taken into consideration before finally deciding what areas of Herb-growing are the best for you, but you can be sure, whatever your circumstances, there will be some Herbs you can grow, and at least one market—probably more —which you can supply.

When planning what markets you intend supplying, the location of your home and land has to be considered.

Giving scope for a wide variety of skills and interests is the growing and marketing of fresh culinary Herbs for restaurants. You will need to be close (say less than 30 miles—50 kilometers) to a town which has a number of good (and preferably expensive) restaurants. The size of the town is unimportant. What *is* important to you is the number of restaurants of this type in the town. They are the ones that will be willing to pay good prices for such hard-to-get items as fresh Herbs. So a town that attracts tourists at the same season of the year as you achieve your peak growing periods is ideal.

Chives and Parsley will be your biggest sellers. The demand for most perennial Herbs will be comparatively small, except for French Tarragon, which will always find a ready market. Dill may be needed in large quantities, but most other annual Herbs will be less in demand.

If you want to retail potted plants, dried Herbs, and other products, you will need to be located on a good road (or at least have access to a good road) where you can put up a sign to indicate how to reach your place. You will have to be willing to meet and serve the public whenever they come to you. Your location is less important if

you are selling your products wholesale. You will deliver them to
your retail outlets, and the public will go to them—not to you.

If you would rather do more field work and deal less with the
public, perhaps the culinary and medicinal dried Herb market
would be better for you. Your climate would need to be mild
enough to give you two or three cuts each year, and you would have
to be able to irrigate.

If you are looking for less gardening and more indoor work,
Catnip toys for the pet shops are a possibility. A few dozen Catnip
plants, some strong cotton material, and a sewing machine are all
you need. Novelty and gift items, too, can be made with the more
fragrant Herbs. If your skills are culinary rather than artistic, how
about a line of gourmet salad dressings?

If your business is being done by mail order, and if you are selling
plants, then you should be located within, say, 10 miles (16
kilometers) of your bus lines. On the other hand, if you are marketing dried Herbs and Herb products, you need only consider the
distance to your nearest post office.

No matter how little or how much land you have, how it lies, or
what rainfall or sunshine is available, there will be some Herb or
Herbs that you can grow profitably.

If you only have a small garden in which to grow your Herbs, you
should choose those that give a large yield of plant material per
square foot of space which they occupy. Rosemary bushes do this,
and with the leaves and flowers you could make hair preparations.
Lavender bushes, from their third year of life onwards, will give a
heavy yield of flowers, which can be used in the making of many
fragrant gift items. The shorter your growing season and the smaller
your growing area, the greater will be the necessity for you to
process and create attractive articles for sale if you are to make good
profits. This work can be done in the off season, and your maximum
output should be timed to meet the Christmas market.

You may be located in an area where winters are long and summers cool. You could specialize in the growing of Angelica, another
heavy producer per square foot. Your end product would be candied Angelica stems and dried leaves to sell for teas, and as a sugar
extender.

In an area with no frosts and long, hot summers, it would be
possible to grow several Herbs that in areas which are not frost free
need greenhouse protection. Bay, Rose Geranium, and Lemon Verbena are examples of Herbs which grow easily and prolifically in
such an area.

Your end-product would be plants which could be shipped in late spring to areas which have a short frost-free growing season. Bay and Lemon Verbena leaves can be dried and marketed for culinary use.

Although many Herbs need as good a rainfall as a vegetable garden, there are a few which will thrive—and even have a more intensive perfume—in a dry climate. Lavender is one of these, and there are markets for it in many forms.

If your garden lacks sunshine, grow Sweet Cicely in the shady places; dry it and package it to be sold as a sugar extender. A damp, shady spot would grow Sweet Woodruff, which is used as snuff as well as in some wines. A dry, rocky area on a hillside or on uneven ground could grow Garden Thyme. It could be dried and mixed with Parsley (grown in your vegetable garden), and Bay (which would have to be bought if your climate is not suitable for growing it), to make "Bouquet Garni," a blend of flavoring Herbs which is in great demand.

So whatever your climate, location, or soil; whatever your interests and skills; no matter if you have a small garden or acres of land—whatever area of Herb-growing and marketing you want to get into, your first need will be for Herb plants, and the raw material they will supply you with.

So let's get on with the preparation of the soil, so that you can plant the Herbs you need—and make them pay.

BORAGE (*Borago officinalis*)

4

CHAPTER 2

Getting Ready

Your first consideration will be to decide what land you can use to grow your Herbs, and how to lay out your beds in such a way that you can work them with the minimum of walking, fetching, and carrying. The "ideal" area would be flat, with no trees, bushes, or other obstacles on it. Whether it is half an acre or only 50 feet square, it can produce Herbs profitably. Read the book through carefully, picking out the areas of Herb-growing which suit you and your garden best, taking into consideration the markets that are open to you.

Tools and Machinery

MINIMUM BASIC HAND TOOLS NEEDED

Spade	Exacto or	Trowel
Iron rake	Stanley knife	Small hand fork
Flat-tined fork	Pruning shears	Soil loosener
Bamboo lawn rake	(good quality)	Any other small
Hoe	Lever-nozzle hose	garden tools you
Dutch or scuffle hoe	(hose gun)	find useful
Half-moon edger		
Wheelbarrow or garden cart		

VARIOUS OTHER TOOLS

Soil sieves—large, free standing (if you have no shredder)
Soil sieves—hand size, including old coarse kitchen sieves!
Seed flats—standard measurement

Pots, plastic—2¼-inch (tall) rose pots, 3-inch square, 4-inch square. (Use square pots; they are easier to handle and fill, and are more economical of space.)
Garden string (Polypropylene—does not rot)
Perforated vinyl hoses for sprinkling
Ordinary hoses
Rotating sprinklers } See section this chapter on Irrigation

IF YOU HAVE SUFFICIENT FUNDS!

A *small rototiller* is one of the most useful of tools, and is really a "must" if you have a quarter of an acre or more under cultivation. It not only prepares your soil for planting, but can be used to mix in compost and fertilizers, keep the soil cultivated, and eradicate the weeds.

One which carries the rotor behind the driving wheels is the best, as this avoids compressing the cultivated soil, and leaves no wheel marks. It should also have swivelling handlebars, so that one can walk on the paths and avoid trampling the soil when working (this is particularly important when you have a heavy soil). The American *Troy-Bilt* and the English *Howard Rotavator* have these good points, and are sturdy, reliable machines.

A *compost shredder*. There are many makes on the market, some with gasoline and some with electric motors. Besides shredding compost, this machine is invaluable for thoroughly mixing all the ingredients for potting soil mixes.

Greenhouse, Potting Shed, and Lath House

In deciding whether you will need a *greenhouse*, your climate has to be considered, and also to some extent the markets which you wish to supply. If you are blessed with an early spring free of frosts, you are lucky indeed. If, on the other hand, your spring is late and you can expect frosts as late as mid May, a greenhouse will be essential if you want to grow Herb plants for sale. It would also be an asset for supplying many of the other markets, as suggested in Chapter 6.

The size of the greenhouse you put up will depend primarily on how much you can afford to spend, and to a certain extent what markets you want to grow for. The smallest "standard" house is five by eight feet, and this is small, though better than nothing. Ours was 14 by 30 feet, with a hot water heating system. The furnace was oil-fired, thermostatically controlled, and entirely automatic. It was a very efficient, labor saving, and trouble-free system.

We seldom had a square inch of bench space to spare between January and mid-May. Had the house been any bigger, it would have been too much to look after, with all the outside work to do as well. So let us say a house somewhere between these two sizes—as big as you can afford. Have your heating arrangements as labor saving as possible. Whatever it costs, avoid a wood- or coal-burning furnace, since this would mean at least one trip to stoke up in the middle of the night, in winter!

This brings me to another important point—*where* to build the greenhouse. On one hand, close to your own dwelling is pleasant when the weather is bad, and, if the greenhouse is small, it might be possible to combine the heating with the house heating system. On the other hand, you may find it more convenient to have it where the other outbuildings are located, and to create a working center arranged to eliminate as much carrying and walking as possible. Of course the terrain will have to be taken into consideration when making these plans.

If there is already a greenhouse on the property, you will have to put up with any inconveniences caused by its siting. If the plumbing and heating arrangements are inadequate, go ahead to improve them. And if you put up any other buildings, be sure to consider their siting in relation to the greenhouse.

Greenhouse building and maintenance is a subject beyond the scope of this book, but there are many good handbooks on the subject. Help should also be sought from the appropriate authorities in government horticultural departments.

Your *potting shed* should be alongside the greenhouse, preferably connected to it and on the same level. Steps are a menace in this area, as I well know—we had three up out of the potting shed into the greenhouse, and three to the outside, because the shed floor was at a lower level than the garden and the greenhouse! The layout of this shed should be planned carefully, with benches at two heights—some at a convenient height to work at standing, and others to sit at.

If the furnace can be housed in the potting shed, you will have a pleasantly warm and dry place to do your plant potting and propagation. This avoids the temptation to work in the greenhouse itself in order to keep warm, and it should never be used as a workshop. A messy greenhouse encourages disease.

There should be running water here too, with at least one sink. The old-fashioned shallow porcelain type is ideal, as seed flats and plants can be watered "from below" (see Chapter 3, "How to Start Herb Plants from Seed Indoors"). If you can put in a second sink, do so. Your floor should be of cement, with a slight slope to a floor drain. Plumbing for the sink need not be elaborate, in fact, the usual U-bend and outlet pipe are not needed. Fix a flexible piece of piping to the outlet of the sinks, and have a floor drain close by. This will avoid problems caused by soil filling the U-bends.

A *lath house*, or *shade house* as it is sometimes called, is invaluable for holding plants ready for sale, or those which are being "hardened off" prior to planting out. It is also an excellent place to set up your shop for selling plants. As there will be a lot of traffic between the lath house and greenhouse, they should be situated close to each other to save any unnecessary extra steps when carrying flats of plants. One appreciates its nearness when the time comes to move plants in late spring (when the greenhouse becomes too hot for them), and again when the plants have to be returned from the lath house, before the winter comes.

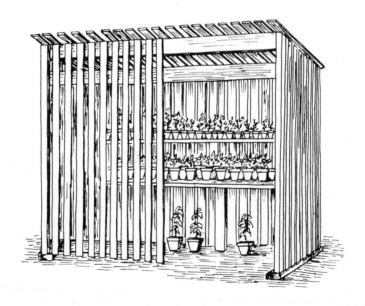

A Lath house

Again, the size of the lath house depends on what you can afford, but do make it at least as big as your greenhouse. Don't forget that plenty of bench space will be needed. Some lath houses can double as extra winter and spring protection if covered with plastic, though with the present price of plastic this might not be an economical proposition. The plastic will have to be removed before the heat of summer—so that the house can once again be used for shade and then renewed the following fall. Whether you do this or not depends on whether the extra expense is warranted by your needs. It might be a temporary help for a year or two, until you can build extra permanent protection.

Initial Preparation of the Soil

There are three possibilities you have to start with. Either your land has never been worked, it has been worked and neglected, or (if you are very lucky), it has been worked and looked after.

1. If your land has never been worked, you will first have to clear most trees, bushes, and other obstructions away. Leave a few trees around the edge of the land—it will prevent too utilitarian an appearance, and give shade. Then, get a professional with a rotary plow to do the initial breaking of the soil, going over the ground twice, but not more—you do not want it pulverized excessively.
2. If it has been worked but neglected, you may be able to handle it yourself with a small rototiller. Try it, and if it overtaxes your machine (and/or you!), get in a professional.
3. If you are so fortunate as to inherit a piece of land that has been well looked after, you will be able to handle it with your rototiller, or even with a fork and a pair of strong arms.

Laying Out the Beds

The suggestions here are designed to make the working of your land as easy and untiring as possible, and to make all the beds accessible in all weathers.

1. Measure the area you have available, and if possible, square it off.
2. Cut four stakes 18 inches (45 cm.) long from 1 x 2's, for each bed, and paint them white. These will be the corner markers of your beds, and later you will have to paint numbers on them. If each bed is marked clearly, it is a great help in keeping records and making your garden plans.
3. Beds should then be marked out about 50 feet (15 m.) long. If they are made any longer, one tends to jump across them (as it's a long walk around), and plants get damaged. Visitors will copy you too, and results are often disastrous.
4. These beds should be made 48 inches (1.20 m.) wide. This enables one to work from either side without standing on the cultivated soil.
5. One of the white stakes should be driven into each corner of the beds. Sink at least half of the length into the ground, hammering it home securely.
6. If possible, leave a 72-inch (1.80 m.) path all around the outside of the laid-out beds, to accommodate machinery, wheelbarrows, etc., and generally to facilitate working.
7. The paths between the beds can either be scraped bare and kept that way, or allowed to grass over, and kept cut with a small mower, the beds edged with a good edging tool. We did the latter. Grass paths give a very neat and workmanlike appearance to the whole garden, provided they are kept well trimmed and edged.

Nature abhors a vacuum, and you may find that the grass soon appears without any help. If it doesn't, grass seed can be sown. Get advice as to the mix from your local Agricultural Extension Service. You want a hard-wearing, slow-growing combination.

Grassed paths keep the sprinkler hoses clean and free from mud, and you yourself do not get muddied when watering. When working on the beds, it is very pleasant to be able to kneel on a grassy sward, instead of in hot, dusty soil.

How to Make Compost

So many books and articles have been written on compost-making that I hesitate to give advice. However, we developed a fairly "lazy"

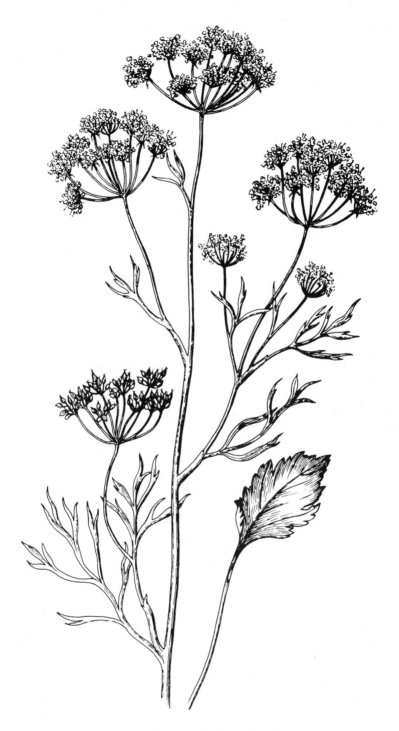

ANISE (*Pimpinella anisum*)

way to do it, so if you haven't already a favorite way of making it, try this one or read *Let it Rot!,* by Stu Campbell, and follow his methods.

The first two essentials for making compost are a "bin" with slatted sides, to allow for ventilation, and a roof to keep off the rain. It is advisable, if you are starting from "scratch," to put up four or even six bins in two lines, back to back. This should give you enough room to keep a steady flow of compost coming. Fill two the first year, and by the time these are ready (in a year to eighteen months), your other bins will be filling up. Then the first compost can be used, and you will have two empty bins again—and so on.

Start the heap with garden waste which is too coarse to pass through your shredder easily (stalks, thick roots, etc.). This will keep the shredded material off the floor of the heap and assist aeration. On top of this base almost any plant material, preferably shredded, can be placed. Exceptions are weeds with creeping roots—especially the Bindweeds and Creeping Jenny, and others belonging to the *Convolvulaceae* family, and Couch, Quack, or Twitch grass (*Agropyren repens*). Any fresh manure you can obtain, rot down in your heap. While building your heap, add a light sprinkling of agricultural or Dolomite lime every 6 or 8 inches. Add seaweed and *raw* vegetable kitchen wastes (not meat or cooked food, as they will encourage rats). Comfrey is worth growing just for the heap, and a stand of Winter Rye, cut in the early summer when still green, is good. Keep the heap damp by running a sprinkler on it occasionally, and punch holes for ventilation right through the heap with an iron bar or pipe. Keep it covered with old sacks. This will help to prevent it from drying out.

Some people insist that heaps should be turned at least once, but we never did. The compost may take six months longer to make, but is far less work. If any unrotted material is found as the heap is being used, it can be put onto another heap to continue rotting. As a new heap is being built up, a thin layer of compost from a heap which has matured, will accelerate the rotting by inoculating the new heap. If Herbal compost accelerators are used, follow the directions of the makers.

If, for some reason, your facilities for making compost are limited, or you are unable to make sufficient, find out if dried steer manure (the composted type if possible) is available in your garden shops or farm stores. This comes in 40-pound plastic sacks, is clean to handle, weed free, and reasonably priced if bought in ton lots.

About Fertilizers and Compost

This is a touchy subject! There are devotees of the organic and inorganic methods, and though in the past these two methods seemed so far apart, it seems to me that the less rabid supporters of each method are beginning to see the others' point of view. I do not think that any experienced and successful gardener will deny that any soil which is to be productive, *must* contain plenty of humus— or that too much humus can be incorporated in the soil. However well-made the compost, additional fertilizers are also necessary. But here the big difference of opinion rears its head!

The supporters of organic methods insist on only "natural" fertilizers—hoof and horn, bone meal, blood meal, phosphate rock, greensand, seaweed, animal manure, and, of course, vegetable residues in the form of compost. Many of these products are getting more and more scarce, and the organic gardener will be hard put to keep up the fertility of his soil, and to replace all the nutrients that intensive production takes out of it.

Intensive gardening is not nature's way. Your plants, in any garden, take far more out of the soil than plants growing in the wild. You are repeatedly cropping from the same piece of land, in a way that nature does not.

Some plants will survive and crop well (providing that the ground is properly prepared and nourished before they are planted) without any supplementary "artificial" fertilizers. But a crop like Chives needs them. It is in the same soil for several years, and continuously produces cut after cut. Your soil's nutrients are going to be depleted, and yields will suffer unless the nutrients are replaced. Nutrients are also leached out of the soil in areas of heavy rainfall.

So I would say, make every effort to obtain as much organic fertilizer and compost as possible. The ideal combination is plenty of organic matter incorporated in the soil, plus long-lasting natural fertilizers to keep your soil producing commercially. But *do* supplement with artificial fertilizers rather than deprive your soil of what it lacks.

These small amounts of chemical fertilizers act like a tonic. Follow manufacturers' instructions on the bag, and weigh or measure accurately the amounts recommended. The gardener who only uses artificial fertilizers and who does not worry about the humus in his soil is piling up trouble for himself. These artificial fertilizers should be regarded as a supplement to your well-nourished, composted soil. Remember that *they are not a substitute for humus.*

When transplanting into the garden or into pots, "transplanting shock" can be lessened by watering with a little *Ra-pid-gro"* or 20-20-20 in solution (follow directions on the bag or can). Organic gardeners can use a little *well-diluted* liquid manure.

Final Preparation
of the Soil

Your soil has been roughly prepared by one or other of the methods suggested in "The Initial Preparation of the Soil," and your beds are marked with stakes. Now is the time to decide what is going to be planted in each bed, for although the basic preparation is the same for each bed, a few plants have special needs, and these can be catered to when doing the final preparations.

The first thing to ascertain is whether your soil needs lime, and how much. A soil test will be necessary to find this out, and your Agricultural Extension Office probably has facilities for doing this for you. Follow their advice. This office is listed in the telephone book under "County Government."

You are aiming to get a soil which will be friable, fertile, and easy to work. If you are using a small garden tiller, first read the manufacturer's instructions and follow them. This may seem an unnecessary suggestion, but you would be surprised how many people keep their instruction book in the house and never refer to it! In case you have lost your instruction book, here are a few suggestions.

If it seems necessary to go over the soil several times to achieve the right texture, start with the machine set for shallow cultivation and deepen it at each run over; this will avoid straining you or your machine. This is the time also to incorporate compost and fertilizer in the soil. You can walk directly behind the machine until the final run over, then the handles should be swivelled to one side, so that you can walk on the path. It is possible that a final raking over may still be necessary—certainly it will if you are going to plant seeds. However, if plants are going in, then this final raking step may possibly be omitted. It all depends on how skilled you have been with the rototiller.

Once this final raking and/or rotavating has been done, *do not walk on the beds*. This will avoid compacting the soil, and will reduce the necessity for too-frequent cultivation—which will bring the weed seeds up from below and encourage their germination. The soil will retain its friability, and established weeds will lift out easily.

You will therefore find that further use of the rototiller for cultivation is unnecessary when growing in these small, intensively planted beds. I am not referring to growing field crops. Those techniques are quite different and are not within the scope of this book.

There should not be any weeds left after all this work is done. However, it sometimes happens that there is a time lapse between making the final preparation and the planting out of the bed. So, just before you plant, go over the bed (kneeling on the path), and lift out any weeds which have appeared, being careful to get all of the roots out.

If you have no rototiller of your own to help with the final preparation of the soil, but have had a professional do the initial breaking and cultivating, you will have to break up the remaining lumps with the back of a spade, removing any weeds with a fork as you go along. Then level the beds with a heavy rake, and remove all the small lumps which won't break down, along with the rubbish and large stones. Finally, rake, rake, and rake again. Add compost and fertilizer, and rake it in; finish all this raking with a lawn rake for a fine finish.

If you have to prepare your beds without any mechanical aids, then the first step will be to dig the ground. Then the levelling and raking should be done as in the previous paragraph. It is hard work though, so try to get some powered help to do the initial breaking of the soil. Whatever method you are using to obtain your friable soil, remember that it should *never* be worked when it is wet.

A SPECIAL NOTE ABOUT COUCH GRASS

This is a troublesome weed in many parts of the world. It is known by several other names, including Quack grass, Twitch grass, Witch grass, Quick grass, Scotch Quelch, and Dog grass. Its Latin name is *Agropyrum repens*, though *Triticum repens* is sometimes used also. Its slender roots creep along just under the surface and branch laterally, nodes spaced about an inch apart producing leaf buds and fine branching roots. The plant should be loosened with a fork, and all its many branches lifted with care, since any piece left in the soil will reproduce itself rapidly. This weed should be cleared from small areas by hand. Some authorities maintain that continuous rototilling will eventually eliminate it, but we did not find this so. There are, of course, specific weed killers for Couch grass, but we did not care to use them. _Don't put the roots on your compost heap. Burn them._

Insects and Diseases

A Herb garden is seldom bothered by insects or disease. In fact, Herbs discourage insects in your garden. Mints, however, may be attacked by rust spots. If they are, dig them up and burn them, for there is no remedy.

Occasionally on Herbs grown indoors, you will find the usual bugs from which many house plants suffer. Read Helen and John Philbrick's _The Bug Book: Harmless Insect Control_ if you have problems.

Soil Mixes

When starting plants from seed and when growing plants in pots, either for sale or for later transplanting into your own garden, it is advisable to make specific soil mixes for each stage of development of the plants.

The base of all good soil mixes is a sterile loam, which is not always easy to find. Small bags of soil mixes are available in most garden shops, but are much too expensive to use on a commercial scale. If you can find a large nursery, which will allow you to buy sterilized loam by the truckload, or even by the cubic yard, this is your best bet, but you may not find anyone willing to do so. We obtained ours through a large grower whom we supplied with specialized plants which he did not grow himself, and he sold us sterilized soil by the truckload at a time of year when he didn't need all he was able to sterilize.

Before your soil arrives, spread a large sheet of six mil plastic and have the truck empty the soil on top. Keep it covered with another

BASIL, SWEET (*Ocimum basilicum*)

17

sheet, weighted down with rocks or two by fours, to prevent soil from blowing away, and to prevent windblown weed seed from getting into it.

If you have a shredder, use it to mix the ingredients for your soil mixes. Though not essential for this job, it produces a more even mix than you can make by hand, and it lightens your work, too.

The other two ingredients for your soil mix are *peat moss* (nursery grind), and coarse, washed, clean *builder's sand*. (Avoid sand impregnated with sea salt.) Sand will also be needed when propagating. To these basic ingredients add in varying amounts ground limestone (preferably Dolomite), superphosphate, sulphate of potash, and hoof and horn meal.

The following tables will give you the quantities to mix for various stages of seed and plant growth. All are based on recommendations by the John Innes Institute of Great Britain.

A bushel is a measure of capacity which equals 4 pecks (32 quarts). In practice, we found gallon antifreeze cans useful for measuring the soil, peat, and sand. An accurate kitchen scale or postal scale is necessary for weighing the fertilizers.

Eight gallon cans, full, equal one bushel. (All measurements below have been converted from Imperial to U.S. gallons.)

To make 3 bushels of John Innes potting compost, mix:

17½ gallon cans of sterilized soil with
 7½ gallon cans of fine (nursery grind) peat moss and
  5 gallon cans of builder's sand. Add to this
  2 ounces of ground limestone and
 12 ounces of base fertilizer (see below)

To make 5 pounds of John Innes base fertilizer, mix:

 2 pounds hoof and horn with
 2 pounds superphosphate and
 1 pound of sulphate of potash
     Store in a dry place, in an airtight container

To make 1 bushel of John Innes seed sowing compost, mix:

 5 gallon cans of sterilized soil with
2½ gallon cans of fine (nursery grind) peat moss and
2½ gallon cans of builder's sand. To this add
1½ ounces of superphosphate
 ¾ ounce of ground limestone

Note that if you have to move plants from their original pots into bigger sizes, the potting compost should have *double* the amount of the basic fertilizer mixed into it—this is called *John Innes Number 2 potting compost*. Plants going into even bigger pots or window boxes to spend most of their life, should be put into *John Innes Number 3 potting compost*, which has *three* times the basic fertilizer.

Organic gardeners, who will not even use this amount of fertilizer, should mix the soil, peat and sand in the recommended amounts, with the limestone and the hoof and horn. Water your young plants with a weak solution of cow manure. But do please use sterilized soil, or you are likely to run into all sorts of troubles— weed seeds germinating and swamping your seedlings or soil-borne diseases. Remember that growing plants in pots is *not* nature's way of doing it!

Irrigation

No matter what your rainfall, you will need to set up efficient methods of irrigation. To grow most herbs intensively and commercially you *must* be able to have water when *you* need it, to produce your crops ready for marketing at the time that you want them. I am not suggesting that you can go against nature, and produce anything and everything out of season (though much can be done which is completely "unnatural"), but I am suggesting that you can give nature a little helping hand to make things more profitable for you.

There are a number of irrigation systems available to you if you have piped water. City water, though at times expensive to use, at least has the advantage of being available year 'round. The exception is during periods of drought when restrictions on water use sometimes come into force—so consider a supplementary source of supply.

If you are fortunate enough to have an all-year stream running through your property, you could use a *hydraulic ram* (a very old invention) to pump water to a storage tank, from which it would be piped to where it is needed. Its only moving parts are a pair of valves, and operating costs are nil. I have seen hydraulic rams in Argentina which are still in operation after more than 50 years of continuous use. Rife Hydraulic Engine Manufacturing Co., Box 367, Millburn, New Jersey, 07401, are manufacturers. Send 50 cents for their installation manual.

A *windmill* can also be used to pump water at very low cost from a well to a storage tank. Major United States manufacturers are Aermotor Water Systems, Division of Braden Industries Inc., Broken Arrow, Oklahoma, 74012, and Dempster Industries Inc., P.O. Box 848, Beatrice, Nebraska, 68310. An excellent book dealing with the above subjects is *New Low-Cost Sources of Energy for the Home*, by Peter Clegg.

To make use of a pond or reservoir as a water supply, you will need a small gasoline- or electric-powered pump to take the water where you need it.

You will have to choose a water distributing system according to your garden's needs and your available cash. One of the simplest, and which we found the most effective for small-scale work with the strip beds, is a soft vinyl sprinkler hose. You can start with two or three, and as you can afford them, add to that number, so that eventually every bed which needs watering will have its own hose. This avoids the constant moving of the hoses, which can not only cause wear and tear on the hoses, but can easily damage the plants in the beds.

One can also restrict the watering to individual beds, and keep it off others which do not require watering. These hoses make the most of the water you use by putting it where you need it. Conversely, the pressure can be raised to water several beds at once if you wish to. These hoses also have the advantage of working efficiently where water pressure is low.

The rotating "Rainbird" sprinkler head, a particularly efficient brand, is excellent for large areas, and can be adjusted to throw an arc of water where you want it. For field-type planting (rather than beds), it is ideal.

Canvas soaker hoses, another type available, we did not find as good as the "sprinkler" hoses. They tended to clog with soil. But this could have been because our soil was a fairly heavy loam. Possibly they would be better on a lighter, sandy soil. It might be worth trying one if *your* soil is light and sandy.

When you water, *soak* the soil. Frequent light surface waterings are wasteful—they do not penetrate to the roots, which is where the water is needed.

Because the topsoil looks dry, it doesn't necessarily mean that water is needed. Poke your fingers well into the soil, and if it is dry three or four inches down, *then* water. Of course, if the plants are wilting, they need water.

One time when more frequent water is usually needed is after transplanting, though if you will follow the suggestions in Chapter 3, "Planting Out Your Herb Plants," and "puddle" them in, they are unlikely to wilt at all.

It is difficult to lay down hard and fast rules to guide you in your watering. In time, by trial and error, you will develop a feel for your plants' needs. Incidentally, if you have made grass paths as suggested in "Laying out the Beds," you will find that they will help to conserve the moisture in these beds.

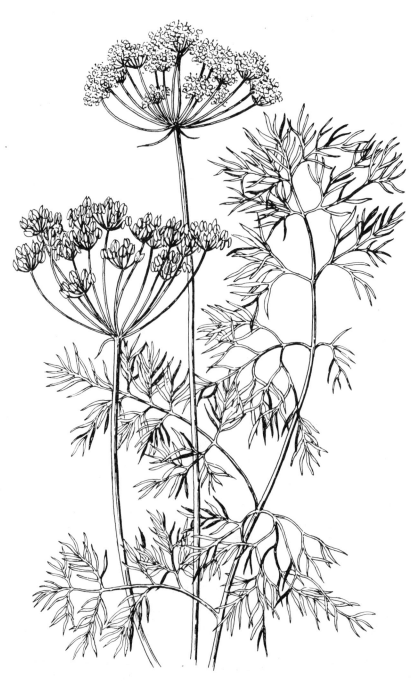

CARAWAY (*Carum carvi*)

CHAPTER 3

Starting Your Herb Garden

It would be very expensive to buy enough plants to start you on a commercial scale, so start as many as possible from seed yourself. However, there are a few important Herbs which cannot be started from seed, and these must be bought as plants (see List A).

There are some Herbs which are slow to germinate and slow to grow. Buy some of these, and try your hand at starting more from seed (see List B).

Some others, though difficult to start, are quite quick-growers once they germinate. Buy a few and grow more from seed, or depend entirely on your own skill in germinating them, and don't buy plants (see List C).

All the annuals, two of the biennials, and two of the perennials should be started from seed (see List D); there is no point in buying plants. A note about customers: you will always find that there will be some who want these plants in pots—people who do not have the facilities to start their own—so it is worth potting up a few for these customers, as well as all the others in Lists A, B, and C. There are two important Herbs which can only be started from cloves or bulbs (see List E).

Note: in the next section, under the heading "Quantity to Buy," the number of plants suggested is the *minimum* number you should buy to get started. Buy more if you can afford them, and if you are in a hurry to build up stock of any particular Herbs.

THE 32 HERBS YOU WILL NEED
TO STOCK YOUR BASIC HERB GARDEN

Herb	List	Page
Angelica (*Angelica archangelica*)	C	34
Anise (*Pimpinella anisum*)	D	40
Basil; Sweet (*Occimum basilicum*)	D	42
Borage (*Borago officinalis*)	D	42
Caraway (*Carum carvi*)	D	40
Catnip (*Nepeta cataria*)	D	38
Chervil (*Anthriscum cerefolium*)	D	42
Chives (*Allium schoenoprasum*)	B	28
Comfrey (*Symphytum peregrinum*)	A	25
Coriander (*Coriandrum sativum*)	D	42
Dill (*Anethum graveolens*)	D	44
Fennel (*Foeniculum vulgare*)	D	38
Garlic (*Allium sativum*)	E	46
Garlic Chives (*Allium tuberosum*)	B	30
Lavender (*Lavandula officinalis*)— Tall-growing varieties	A	25
Lavender (*Lavandula officinalis*)— Dwarf and Semi-Dwarf varieties	B	30
Lemon Balm (*Melissa officinalis*)	C	36
Marjoram, Sweet (*Marjorana hortensis*)	D	44
Mint, English (*Mentha cordifolia*)	A	26
Mint, Pepper (*Mentha piperita*)	A	26
Oregano (*Origanum vulgare*)	C	36
Parsley (*Carum petroselinum*)	D	40
Rosemary (*Rosmarinus officinalis*)	B	32
Sage (*Salvia officinalis*)—Broad leaf	A	26
Sage (*Salvia officinalis*)—Narrow leaf	D	40
Savory, Summer (*Satureia hortensis*)	D	44
Savory, Winter (*Satureia montana*)	B	34
Shallots (*Allium ascalonicum*)	E	46
Sweet Cicely (*Myrrhis odorata*)	C	38
Tarragon, French (*Artemisia dracunculus*)	A	26
Thyme, Garden (*Thymus vulgaris*)	B	34
Thyme, Lemon (*Thymus citriodorus*)	A	28

How to Grow the 32 Basic Herbs

LIST A

Comfrey, Russian (*Symphytum perigrinum*). It is a hardy perennial growing some 24 to 36 inches (1.20 to 1.50 m.) high. It grows well in a clay soil. Lighter soils need constant manuring to achieve heavy growth. It will tolerate any fresh manure—in fact, thrives on it. It is propagated by offsets or pieces of root with a bud attached—in fact, any piece of root will grow.

Plant out from early spring to fall, watering young plants if the location is dry. It should be planted away from the rest of the Herb garden in an area of its own. In a few years you can have many plants that will give you heavy crops for making compost.

Quantity to buy: 20 pieces of root. Plant them 36 inches (90 cm.) apart.

Note: Recently I have seen seed of Comfrey advertised. This is *Symphytum asperum* (not *S. perigrinum*).

See Appendix E for specialist growers of plants, and for a book about Comfrey production see Appendix D.

Lavender (*Lavandula officinalis*). Tall-growing varieties. There are two main types of tall-growing Lavenders, the Mitcham and Grey Hedge types, (within these two types there are several varieties). It would be pointless to suggest that one or the other should be selected, as different districts have different varieties which are most suitable to their climates and soils.

These Mitcham and Hedge types grow about 30 inches (75 cm.) high, requiring a light, well-drained soil, and full sun. Previous liming is advisable. Propagation should be carried out by cuttings from two inches (5 cm.) to four inches (10 cm.) long, as soon as the new growth has attained that length, either in early summer or after harvesting, in early fall. The dwarf and semi-dwarf (see List B) are faster growing.

Lavender is distilled and used in the perfume and cosmetics industry.

Quantity to Buy: Two, preferably different varieties. Plant 36 inches (90 cm.) apart.

Mints. All Mints are hardy perennials. Start with the two varieties listed below.

Most of the Mints grow to a height of about 36 inches (90 cm.). They need rich, though not freshly manured, soil. Some shade is preferable, though if the ground retains moisture well it is not essential. Propagation is by runners, although cuttings can also be taken.

English or **Lamb Mint** (*Mentha cordifolia*) is an excellent early Mint. It has crinkly, almost heart-shaped leaves, and an excellent flavor. It may be hard to find, but is well worth looking for.

Quantity to Buy: 10 to 20 pieces of root. Plant 18 inches (45 cm.) apart.

Peppermint (*Mentha piperita crispula*). This is the curly-leaved Peppermint. The leaves are very dark with purple tones, and the stems are purple too. It smells rather strong when fresh, but dried its flavor is excellent. The cultivation is the same as for any other Mints. It is used in medicine, for flavoring, and in the cosmetic, perfume and liqueur industries.

Quantity to buy: 20 to 30 pieces of root. Plant 18 inches (45 cm.) apart.

Sage (*Salvia officinalis*). It is necessary to buy plants only if you want the broad-leaved non-flowering type, sometimes called Holt's Mammoth. Sage is a hardy perennial, grows about 18 inches (45 cm.) tall, likes sandy, well-limed soil, and plenty of sun. It can be propagated by layering or cuttings. It is used in the kitchen, in medicine, and by the perfume industry.

Quantity to buy: 2 plants. Planted at least 24 inches (60 cm.) apart.

Tarragon (*Artemisia dracunculus*). This true French Tarragon *cannot* be grown from seed, and those listed in catalogs will be Russian Tarragon (*Artemisia dracunculoides*), which is *useless* in the kitchen. True French Tarragon, a hardy perennial, grows to a height of about 24 inches (60 cm.), (the Russian is taller). The leaves are deep green and glossy, (the Russian paler and willowy). The flavor of the French is warm, aromatic, and slightly "biting," (the Russian negligible).

MINT, PEPPER (*Mentha piperita*)

French Tarragon needs a sunny position, and light, sandy, well-drained soil for rapid growth. In heavier soils it will grow, but more slowly. It is best to propagate it as the new shoots start to show in spring: the plants should be lifted carefully, the soil washed off the roots, and the whole plant gently disentangled. Pieces of root with shoot attached may then be replanted 12 inches (30 cm.) apart. Cut out any rotted root, but leave all the live, succulent root *un*trimmed, and replant.

Note: it is not the cold of winter which will kill French Tarragon, but *dampness,* which rots the roots.

Tarragon, used for flavoring in the kitchen, is one Herb no "gourmet" cook will be without—and everyone is willing to pay for!

Quantity to buy: As many as you can afford. It will be very expensive, because it is slow to grow and difficult to propagate. Take good care of it, because in time it can be a real moneymaker. Plant 12 inches (30 cm.) apart.

Lemon Thyme (*Thymus citriodorus*). This is not an easy plant to find. Be sure you get the bushy one—not just a lemon-scented creeping Thyme. It is a hardy perennial, grows 12 inches (30 cm.) high, has a "softer" growth than the common garden Thyme, and the leaves are paler. It thrives best in a light, dry, well-limed soil, and in full sun. It is propagated by cuttings or by division of the whole plant, which is dug up and torn apart. Any pieces with roots attached can then be replanted 18 inches (45 cm.) apart, burying all the woody stems, and leaving only green leaves above the ground. It can also be layered, but cannot be grown from seed. It is used in cooking, and makes an excellent tea.

Quantity to buy: 3 plants. Plant 18 inches (45 cm.) apart.

LIST B

Chives (*Allium schoenoprasum*). This hardy perennial plant will grow from eight to 12 inches (20 to 30 cm.) high. Preferring a rich, well-composted soil, it will tolerate some shade in summer. Grown commercially it should have full sun. Propagation is by division of the whole plant or by seed. (See Chapter 8, "Growing Chives.")

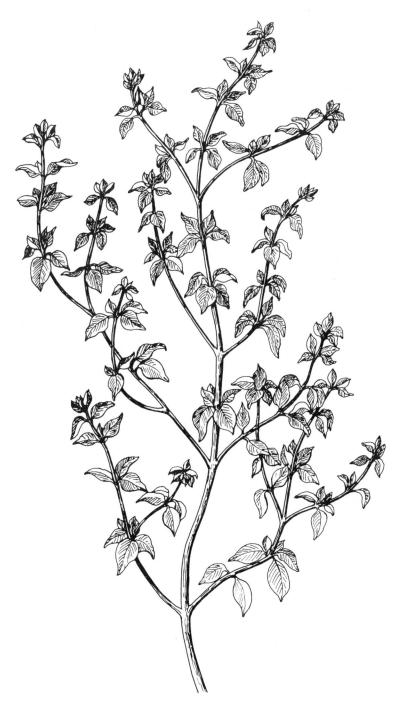

THYME, LEMON (*Thymus citriodorus*)

Two thousand two- or three-year-old plants should be enough to supply approximately 30 to 40 pounds of the fresh Herb each week at the height of the growing season, cutting one-third of the crop each week. This period is usually late spring and very early summer—before the really hot weather comes (when production will fall off, even with good irrigation).

Chives are used for flavoring food, and only when used fresh is the true, full flavor obtained.

Quantity to buy: As many as you can afford—start more from seed. Plant eight inches (20 cm.) apart.

Garlic Chives (*Allium tuberosum*). Like Chives, it is a hardy perennial, but appears a little later in spring. The flower stalks reach a height of 30 inches (75 cm.), though the green leaves are somewhat shorter and triangular. They are not hollow like ordinary Chives. Propagation is by division of the whole plant in spring or early summer, or by seed in spring.

Garlic Chives are used raw in the same dishes in which ordinary Chives are used, but where a Garlic flavor is wanted. They also discourage many insect pests.

Quantity to buy: Three plants—more if you have chefs who are interested in them. Start more from seed. Plant 10 inches (25 cm.) apart.

Lavender (*Lavandula officinalis*)—Dwarf and Semi-Dwarf Varieties. *Lavandula spica* and *Lavandula vera* used to be considered two distinct species. They are now often grouped together as *Lavandula officinalis*. All are hardy perennials.

There are a number of different varieties. I suggest that you start with Mustead Dwarf, which grows about 18 inches (45 cm.) high, and Hidcote Purple, which grows about 12 inches (30 cm.) tall.

They produce the best perfume when grown in soil which is poor and gravelly; they require full sun. Propagation of these dwarf and semi-dwarf varieties can be by seed (which is very slow to germinate, and the plants are very slow-growing), or by cuttings, as early in the year as material becomes available.

But the best and quickest way is by division of three-year-old plants, in spring. They should be lifted and torn apart. Any piece with roots attached should be replanted deeply, so that all the woody stem is buried.

GARLIC CHIVES (*Allium tuberosum*)

The oil distilled from the flowers is used in the perfume and cosmetic industries. It also has medicinal uses.

Quantity to buy: Six of each variety. Plant 24 inches (60 cm.) apart.

Rosemary (*Rosmarinus officinalis*). This perennial will eventually grow to 48 to 60 inches (1.20 to 1.50 m.) in height, if it will stand your winters. Preferring a well-drained, light and well-limed soil and full sun. It can be propagated from cuttings and by layering. Germination of seed and growth of the tiny seedlings is very slow.

There is a beautiful, upright variety called "Miss Jessup," which we found slightly hardier than the ordinary Rosemary. There are several prostrate Rosemarys, none of which is hardy, though *R. officinalis humilis* is the least tender of them.

It is very difficult to say how much frost Rosemary will stand. We found it hardy on southern Vancouver Island in "normal" winters. However, the winter of 1968–69 was exceptionally cold, temperatures dropping as low as zero degrees F. (−18° C.), with bitter winds and periods of alternate thawing and freezing. All our Rosemary plants, which were then between one and five years old, were lost. Yet I know of a very old plantation of Rosemary which remains undamaged in temperatures of 14° F. (−10 C.°); this was high in the sierras of central Argentina, and the atmosphere was very dry.

So I would suggest that you only leave one or two mature plants outside, until you know what your winters will do to them. Take all the others, especially the young ones, into the greenhouse during the cold months. In a winter temperature of 45° F. (7° c.) they will thrive. Be very careful to harden them off slowly in the spring, before you plant them in the garden again.

Rosemary is used for flavor in the kitchen, in medicine, cosmetics—especially in hair preparations—and in the perfume industry.

Quantity to buy: Six, if you can afford them. When you are buying your plants, be sure they are not root-bound in the pots, or they will never really grow well. Grow some from seed, and propagate more from cuttings off your bought plants. Mature plants should stand 36 inches (90 cm.) apart.

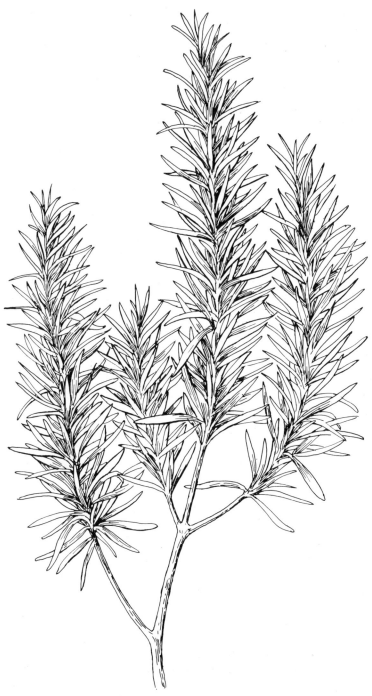

ROSEMARY (*Rosmarinus officinalis*)

33

Savory, Winter (*Satureia montana*). This very hardy perennial grows into a neat bush some eight inches (20 cm.) high. It prefers a poor, well-drained soil and full sun. It may be propagated from seed, which is slow to germinate, by cuttings, by division of the whole plant, or by stool layering.

It is used in the kitchen for flavor, and medicinally.

Quantity to buy: Three. Plant 12 inches (30 cm.) apart.

Thyme, Garden (*Thymus vulgaris*). This is a hardy perennial, though it needs renewal every three to four years, as it gets very woody. It prefers a light, sandy, well-limed and very well-drained soil, and full sun.

There are two equally good varieties of this culinary Thyme. The English, or Winter, which grows some 10 inches (25 cm.) high, is hard to germinate from seed. It can be propagated more easily by cuttings and division of the whole plant. The French, or Summer, which grows about 18 inches (45 cm.) high, on the other hand, germinates easily from seed, which should be sown in late spring. It can also be propagated from cuttings, stool layering and division of the plants. When replanting the divided plants, care should be taken that all the woody stems are buried.

Garden Thyme is used in the kitchen for flavoring, in medicine, and industrially in perfumes, deodorants and insecticides. It is also used in embalming fluids and in preserving specimens.

Quantity to buy: Four, and grow more from seed. Plants need to stand 12 inches (30 cm.) apart.

LIST C

Angelica (*Angelica archangelica*). Though considered to be a biennial, this Herb will often not flower until its third summer, but once it has flowered and seeded, it will die. It may have produced side shoots in its second year, and these will live on. In a moist, rich soil, preferably in partial shade, Angelica will sometimes reach a height of 84 inches (over 2 m.).

It is propagated by seed, which must be fresh and planted in fall. The seedlings are unlikely to appear before the following spring. Once you have established a plant, and it has self-sown its seeds, you will never be without it. If, to get started, you are

SAVORY, WINTER (*Satureia montana*)

able to get a few seedlings when they are *very* small, do so. They transplant quite well, but they *must* be very young, while their roots are less than two inches (5 cm.) long.

Angelica is used in the kitchen, in medicine, and in the perfume, wine and liqueur industries.

Quantity to buy: Six seedlings or two plants. Plant 36 inches (90 cm.) apart.

Lemon Balm (*Melissa officinalis*). A hardy perennial which will grow 48 inches (1.20 m.) high. This delicious, lemon-scented plant is not unlike a small-leaved nettle. It prefers a well-drained, light, sandy soil, full sun or partial shade. It can be propagated by cuttings, by plant division, and by seed. Though the seed is slow to germinate, the resulting plants seem to be the sturdiest—especially when the seed is self-sown. The seedlings, when small, can be lifted and replanted where needed.

There seems to be a misapprehension that Lemon Balm spreads itself like mint—it doesn't. The clumps get larger each year, but I have never seen underground runners—it will not "take over."

Lemon Balm is used in the kitchen when a lemony flavor is required, in medicine, and in the perfume and liqueur industries.

Quantity to buy: Two plants. Start more from seed, or allow these plants to flower and self-sow. Plants should stand 18 inches (45 cm.) apart.

Oregano (*Origanum vulgare*). Also called Wild Marjoram. It is a hardy perennial, growing to about 18 inches (45 cm.) high, prefers a dry, light, well-limed soil, and full sun. It can be propagated by seed, division of the whole plant, and by stem cuttings in spring and in fall, where winters are mild.

If you can locate a good variety of culinary Oregano (often called "Italian") buy plants and propagate from them vegetatively. The flavor will be superior to the common wild *Origanum vulgare*. A low-growing variety known as Greek Oregano is also excellent in the kitchen.

Oregano is used in the kitchen and in medicine. Some strains, when grown in a hot, dry situation, produce such sweet-smelling foliage that they are in demand in the perfume industry.

Quantity to buy: Three plants. Grow more from seed. Plant 18 inches (45 cm.) apart.

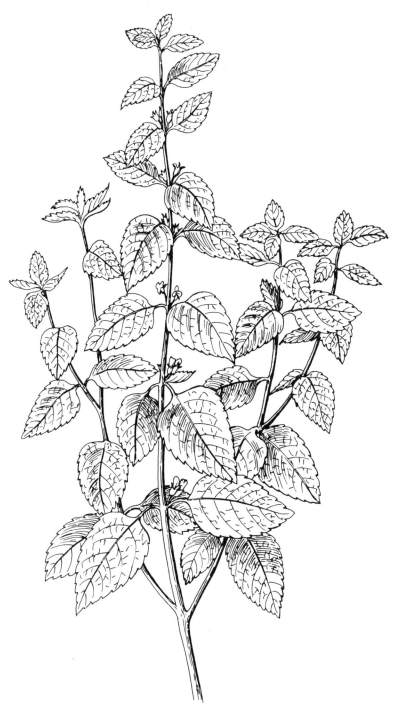

LEMON BALM (*Melissa officinalis*)

Sweet Cicely (*Myrrhis odorata*). A very hardy perennial, growing some 24 inches (60 cm.) high. It likes a rich, moist soil, and partial shade. Though it can be propagated from seed, germination is very slow. Self-sown seed will produce seedlings the spring following the fall sowing. Pieces of root, severed so that each piece has a bud on it, are the easiest way to propagate it. The roots should be dug, cut, and replanted in early spring, as the first leaves begin to show green. The Herb, used in the kitchen to cut down the acidity of fruit, is also marketed to the liqueur industry.

Quantity to buy: Three pieces of root, or three plants, and grow more from seed. Plant 24 inches (60 cm.) apart.

LIST D

Catnip (*Nepeta cataria*). There's no trouble with the germination of this hardy perennial. The theory is that your cats will not worry a new seed bed, but will trample and/or eat your transplanted seedlings. Perhaps our cat had never been told the difference . . . . they liked them all! So protect your beds from the cats . . . . just in case. Plant where it is to grow, and thin out to 12 inches (30 cm.) apart. The plants will reach a height of 36 inches (90 cm.) the second year. For the maximum flavor and smell, plant them in a dry, sandy, sunny situation; however, they will thrive in most soils, except badly drained clay. It is a hardy perennial.

Propagation can also be done by division of the plants, and cuttings. Self-sown seedlings can be transplanted where wanted. I have read that Catnip will sometimes die after flowering, like a biennial, though this was not our experience.

Fennel (*Foeniculum vulgare*). This is another easy perennial to start from seed. Liking a well-limed soil in a sunny spot, it will grow some 60 inches (1.50 m.) high. The seedlings should be thinned to 18 inches (45 cm.) apart.

Seedlings can be transplanted, when very small, into pots for sale, but they grow so fast that only a few should be done at a time. With us it was never a good seller as a plant. (Be careful that you do not get the Sweet Fennel seed, which is an annual, and a vegetable.)

Fennel is used in the kitchen, in medicine, and in the cosmetic and perfume industries.

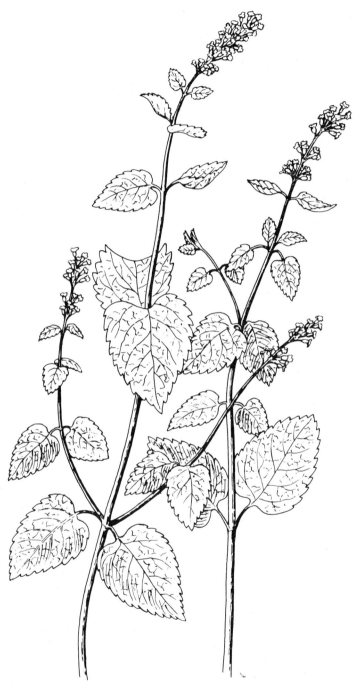

CATNIP (*Nepeta cataria*)

Sage (*Salvia officinalis*). See also under List A. If you are unable to get the non-flowering broad-leaved Sage mentioned under List A, start the flowering type (which is also a hardy perennial) from seed. Germination takes 10 to 14 days in the spring, and the little plants transplant well. Put them 12 inches (30 cm.) apart, and when they grow large enough to touch each other, the alternate plants can be moved, so that they are finally 24 inches (60 cm.) apart. They like sandy, well-drained soil, and plenty of sun. Sage is used in the kitchen for flavor, in medicine, and in the perfume and cosmetic industries.

Caraway (*Carum carvi*) is a biennial which germinates easily. It can be sown in fall to produce the seeds the next year, or a spring sowing one year will produce the seeds the following year. It grows to a height of 24 inches (60 cm.).

Caraway needs an ordinary, well-worked soil, with plenty of sun. The plants should be thinned to eight inches (20 cm.) apart. The seed ripens unevenly, and care must be taken to harvest them all before the first begin to fall. The plants should be cut at ground level, and hung in bunches in a cool, dry place—over paper, to catch the seeds as they fall.

It is used in the kitchen for flavor, in medicine, and by the perfume and cosmetics industries.

Parsley (*Carum petroselinum*), also a biennial, must be started from seed. It needs a rich, well-worked soil, sun or partial shade. Plants should be thinned to eight inches (20 cm.) apart.

Besides being used in the kitchen for flavor, it is used in medicine, and in the garden as an insecticide against onion and carrot fly. The perfume industry extracts an essential oil from its seed.

For full details, see Chapter 7, "Growing Parsley."

The rest of the Herbs in this list are all annuals

Anise (*Pimpinella anisum*). A dainty 24 inches high (60 cm.) plant grown for its seed, needs 120 days of frost-free weather, and should not be sown till the days and nights lose their chill. It requires ordinary, well-worked soil, and full sun. As soon as the seeds begin to ripen, they should be treated like Caraway. Seedlings should be thinned to 4 inches (10 cm.) apart.

SAGE (*Salvia officinalis*)—Broad leaf

41

It is used in the kitchen, in medicine, and in the cosmetic and liqueur industries.

Basil, Sweet (*Ocimum basilicum*). A tender annual; heat loving and frost shy. Basil should be sown in late spring at a *minimum* temperature of 60° F. (15° C.). Germination is quick, especially at higher temperatures. As seedlings tend to "damp off," take preventive measures as outlined later in this chapter.

It grows to a height of 18 inches (45 cm.), needs rich, well-composted soil, and plenty of sun. If you have sown the seed in a greenhouse, do not transplant the young Basil plants into the garden until the nights (as well as the days) are warm. Mature plants should stand 12 inches (30 cm.) apart.

It is used in the kitchen for flavor, in medicine, and in perfumes.

Borage (*Borago officinalis*). In ordinary, well-drained soil, in sun or partial shade, this lovely plant will grow to a height of 36 inches (90 cm.). I have seen one plant cover two square feet (60 sq. cm.) of ground, and have literally hundreds of deep blue flowers on it. So give it room, and it will be a real conversation piece.

Plant seed in late summer, and a rosette of leaves will form. By early summer the next year, the plant will be in full flower. Self-sown seedlings will appear after the first seeding, and there will be no need to sow seed ever again! Leave at least 18 inches (45 cm.) between plants.

Borage is used in the kitchen, and in medicine.

Chervil (*Anthriscum cerefolium*). This delicately flavored annual Herb thrives in cool weather, requires some shade, and an ordinary, well-drained soil. The leaves grow about six inches (15 cm.) high, but the flower heads reach about 18 inches (45 cm.) or taller. Plants from self-sown seedlings will often over-winter successfully. The seed must be fresh to germinate well.

Your first sowing can be made in very early spring. Allow a plant or two to go to seed, and you will be assured of a continuous supply. Seedlings should be thinned to eight inches (20 cm.) apart. Do not transplant, or they will "bolt."

It is used in the kitchen for flavor.

Coriander (*Coriandrum sativum*). This is another annual grown for its flavorsome seeds, though its foliage has an unpleasant smell.

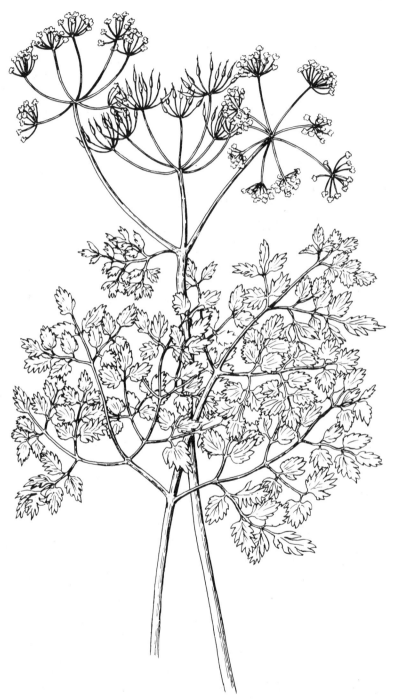

CHERVIL (*Anthriscum cerefolium*)

Plant in late spring (it is quite slow to germinate) in ordinary, well-worked soil and in the sun. It should not be transplanted, but thinned to four inches (10 cm.) apart. It will grow to a height of 36 inches (90 cm.), but often doesn't reach this height. The seed will ripen in late summer to early fall, turning to a fawn color when ripe. The plant should then be cut off at ground level, and laid in a dry, sunny spot to thoroughly dry the seeds.

It is used in the kitchen for its flavor, in medicine and industrially in gin and liqueur production.

Dill (*Anethum graveolens*). This annual plant, which flavors Dill pickles, thrives in a lightish, sandy soil, in full sun. It is quick to germinate. It does not transplant well, and should be thinned out to ten inches (25 cm.) apart. The plant grows to 36 inches (90 cm.) in height, and as it is somewhat "weedy" in growth, winds can do it damage. So, if a sheltered spot is available, use it for your Dill.

It is used in the kitchen for flavor, in medicine, and in the perfume industry.

Marjoram, Sweet (*Marjorana hortensis* or *Origanum marjorana*). Under completely frost-free conditions Sweet Marjoram is perennial, but where there is any frost, it must be treated as a half-hardy annual. It should be started in a temperature of 60° F. (15° C.), and the little plants not put in the garden until *all* risk of frosts is over, and when the nights are beginning to warm up. Follow the directions given later in this chapter, "How to Start Herb Plants from Seed Indoors."

It needs a rich, light, well-worked soil, and a sheltered, sunny position. Plant 12 inches (30 cm.) apart. It grows to a height of 8 to 12 inches (20 to 30 cm.).

Note: When putting up for sale as plants in pots, put three little seedlings in each three-inch square pot; this will give you a salable item quickly.

The Herb is used in the kitchen for flavor, in medicine, and the perfume industry.

Savory, Summer (*Satureia hortensis*). Sow this annual Savory in late spring. It grows to a height of 18 inches (45 cm.), and prefers a light, though enriched soil, and full sun. It does not transplant well, so thin to eight inches (20 cm.) apart.

Used in the kitchen for its flavor, and crushed, it is good in an emergency, to relieve the pain of bee stings.

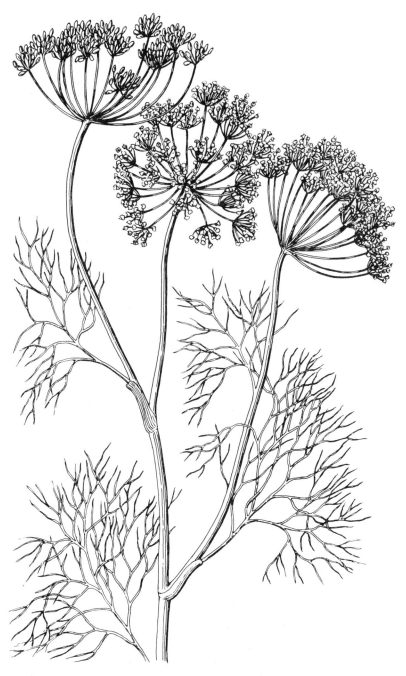

DILL (*Anethum graveolens*)

45

LIST E

Garlic (*Allium sativum*). The bulbs should be gently separated into the little cloves, which can be planted 6 inches (15 cm.) apart, 2 inches (5 cm.) deep, in mid fall or very early spring, in rich, but not freshly manured ground. They like plenty of sun, and a well-drained situation, but should be kept well watered in dry spells, until they begin to ripen. Then water should be withheld. When the leaves have turned yellow, the bulbs should be lifted, and dried in the sun. They are best stored at 60° F. (15° C).

Garlic is used in the kitchen for flavor, and in medicine.

Shallots (*Allium ascalonicum*). When you buy stock for planting, choose small bulbs. Press each bulb into well-worked, well-drained soil. (Unlike Garlic the bulbs cannot be separated into cloves.) Heavy soil is not suitable. Eight inches (20 cm.) should be left between the bulbs. Once rooted, they will not transplant.

Care should be taken when weeding not to disturb the roots. The leaves will start to yellow at the tips in midsummer, and then the soil should be scooped away from the bulbs to allow ripening. When the leaves turn brown, the whole "nest" of bulbs should be lifted and dried in the sun (when possible), or in a temperature of 60° F. (15° C), where there is a current of air, and low humidity.

The larger bulbs should be used for sale, and the smaller ones kept in a cool frost-free place for planting for the next crop.

Buying Plants

When you have located a good Herb farm or nursery, make an appointment to go and visit it. Some farms will have facilities for sending plants by mail or bus, but it is much more satisfactory to go there yourself, even if it means some expense. Remember that you are buying the parents of all your future plants.

Whether you tell them what you are planning to do or not, you will have to decide for yourself. You cannot expect somebody in your own area to welcome competition. On the other hand, they may deal only in wholesale quantities, and be happy to see a retail outlet starting up. They may be glad to find somebody who wants to

WHAT EACH OF THE 32 BASIC HERBS
CAN BE USED FOR

Angelica	Bees, cosmetics, flavor, liqueurs, medicine, perfume, sugar extender, tea
Anise	Cosmetics, flavor, insect repellent, liqueurs, medicine, perfume
Basil, Sweet	Bees, flavor, insect repellent, medicine, perfume
Borage	Bees, flavor, medicine
Caraway	Cosmetics, flavor, liqueurs, medicine
Catnip	Bees, cats, insect repellent, medicine, tea
Chervil	Flavor, medicine
Chives	Flavor
Comfrey	Compost making, medicine, stock feed, as a vegetable
Coriander	Cosmetics, flavor, liqueurs, medicine, perfume
Dill	Bees, cosmetics, flavor, medicine, perfume, tea
Fennel	Bees, flavor, liqueurs, medicine, perfume, tea
Garlic	Flavor, medicine
Garlic Chives	Flavor, insect repellent
Lavenders—Tall and Dwarf	Bees, cosmetics, insect repellent, liqueurs, medicine, perfume
Lemon Balm	Bees, flavor, liqueurs, medicine, perfume, sugar extender, tea
Marjoram, Sweet	Bees, flavor, medicine, perfume, tea
Mint, English	Flavor, liqueurs, medicine, mouse repellent, tea
Mint, Pepper	Flavor, liqueurs, medicine, tea
Oregano	Bees, flavor, medicine, perfume
Parsley	Flavor, insect repellent, medicine
Rosemary	Bees, cosmetics, flavor, insect repellent, medicine
Sages	Bees, cosmetics, flavor, insect repellent, medicine, tea
Savory, Summer	Bees, flavor, medicine
Savory, Winter	Bees, flavor, medicine
Shallots	Flavor
Sweet Cicely	Bees, flavor, liqueurs, sugar extender
Tarragon, French	Cosmetics, flavor, perfume
Thyme, Garden	Bees, cosmetics, flavor, insect repellent, liqueurs, medicine, perfume, tea
Thyme, Lemon	Bees, flavor, tea

specialize in a particular branch of Herb production, and be very helpful. So play it by ear!

If you can visit the farm in the "off" season, so much the better. Visitors are much more welcome when work is not pressing. If you give an order for collection at a later date, *do* offer to pay for it now, or at least leave a *substantial* deposit—say 50 percent.

I know from experience that nothing is more annoying than to have an unpaid order ready on a specified date, and not have it

HOW EACH OF THE 32 BASIC HERBS CAN BE USED

All the Herbs listed for the basic Herb garden will be found in at least one of the lists below

Herbs for a Bee Garden

Angelica
Basil, Sweet
Catnip
Dill
Fennel
Lavenders
Lemon Balm
Marjoram, Sweet
Rosemary
Sages
Savories
Sweet Cicely
Thymes

Herbs for Cosmetics and/or Perfume Industries

Angelica
Anise
Basil, Sweet
Caraway
Coriander
Dill
Fennel
Lavenders
Lemon Balm
Marjoram, Sweet
Rosemary
Sages
Tarragon, French
Thyme, Garden

Herbs Used for Flavor and/or in the Kitchen

Angelica
Anise
Basil, Sweet
Borage
Caraway
Chervil
Chives
Comfrey
Coriander
Dill
Fennel
Garlic
Lemon Balm
Marjoram, Sweet
Mints
Parsley
Rosemary
Sages
Savories
Shallots
Sweet Cicely
Tarragon, French
Thymes

Herbs for Dyes

None

picked up. One goes on holding it just in case the customer turns up, and finally the plants grow too big for the pots and have to be thrown out.

When you collect your plants, ask how recently they have had plant food, and if they haven't during the last ten days, give them a shot of *Ra-pid-gro* when you get them home. Ask if they have been indoors or outside at the nursery. If indoors, be sure to harden them off before you plant them in your garden.

Herbs Used for Teas

Angelica
Catnip
Dill
Fennel
Lemon Balm
Marjoram, Sweet
Mints
Sages
Thymes, Garden and Lemon

Herbs for Repelling Insects

Anise
Basil, Sweet
Catnip
Garlic Chives
Lavenders
Mints
Parsley
Rosemary
Sages
Thyme, Garden

Herbs Used in Liqueurs

Angelica
Anise
Caraway
Coriander
Fennel
Lavenders
Lemon Balm
Peppermint
Sweet Cicely
Thymes, Garden and Lemon

Herbs Used as Sugar Extenders (when cooking acid fruits)

Angelica
Lemon Balm
Sweet Cicely

A Cat Herb

Catnip

Herbs Used in Medicine

Angelica
Anise
Basil, Sweet
Borage
Caraway
Catnip
Chervil
Comfrey
Coriander
Dill
Fennel
Garlic
Lavenders
Lemon Balm
Marjoram, Sweet
Mints
Oregano
Parsley
Rosemary
Savories
Thyme, Garden

Planting Your Herb Plants

Choose a day when the soil is not too wet and the sun is not shining. Spring and early fall are usually the best times, but cool summer days are suitable also.

Holding your plant pot upside down, put the index and third fingers on each side of the stem of the plant. Tap the bottom of the pot gently with a trowel, or tap one edge of the pot on the edge of a table, and the plant, with roots and ball of soil attached, will fall neatly into your hand.

The planting distances at the beginning of this chapter may seem excessive, but they are not. *Don't* crowd your plants. Dig a hole a *little* bigger than the root ball, fill it with water or liquid fertilizer (see Chapter 2, "About Fertilizers and Compost"), allow to drain away, and put the plant in. This is called "puddling" them in. Press soil firmly around the roots, and top up to be level with the surrounding soil. The topsoil should be dry—then the sun will not bake it hard. Remember, it's the *roots* which need the water.

Note that if the plant is very tall or the foliage is very heavy, it will need cutting back. Only practice and familiarity with each variety of Herb will make you a proficient pruner.

A plant with roots and ball of soil attached will fall neatly into your hand.

"Puddling in" a plant

How to trim excess leaf growth. Cut back as indicated by bars.

Keep an eye on the newly planted out stock, and at the first sign of wilting, water the plants. In time you will be able to judge when they are in need of water, and catch them before they droop. When you water plants, give them a good soaking—surface watering does more harm than good.

How to Start Herb Plants
From Seed Outdoors

All annual Herb seeds and also most biennials may be started by
sowing them directly in the garden. Parsley, and all perennial
Herbs, are best sown according to the suggestions in the next
section, "Starting Herbs from Seed Indoors"; the possible exception being Fennel, which can be sown direct, like an annual.

The method for sowing them is the same as for any vegetable:

1. Prepare the seed bed, using a fine rake.
2. Make a *shallow* furrow.
3. Sow the seed very thinly.
4. Cover with the sifted soil to the depth of not more than twice
   the diameter of the seed, and gently tamp the soil down with
   the back of a small rake.
5. Do not allow the seed bed to dry out. Water with a fine spray
   regularly till the first seedlings begin to show.
6. Thin out when the seedlings are an inch or so high. Suggestions as to distances apart, and ways to thin will be found in
   this chapter, "Plants You Will Need to Stock Your Basic Herb
   Garden," and in Chapter 9, "More Herbs to Grow."

How to Start Herb Plants
from Seed Indoors

Depending on the weather, seed may either be started in the greenhouse, lath house, or in a cold frame, in flats, or in pots. Very small
quantities may also be started in the kitchen, but hardening off is
tricky, unless you have "Gro-Lites" or other fluorescent light suitable for your young seedlings. A few seeds, namely Parsley, Sweet
Marjoram, and Lemon Balm, will germinate more easily if soaked in
warm water for 24 hours before planting.

LAVENDER (*Lavandula officinalis*)—
Tall-growing variety

WHEN A LARGE QUANTITY
OF ANY ONE HERB IS NEEDED

1. Fill a standard seed flat with soil mix. (See Chapter 2, "Soil Mixes.")
2. Tamp down gently, so that the soil is half an inch below the top of the flat.
3. Gently shake the seed over the soil, so that it is well spread out. (The only time to sow thickly is when sowing Chives— see Chapter 7, "Growing Chives.")
4. Using a coarse kitchen sieve to sift the soil, lightly cover the seed to barely twice its own depth. Thus, if you are sowing Sweet Marjoram seed, which is very small, very little soil is needed to cover it. If, on the other hand, you are sowing Sage, quite a lot more soil should be used. *Never* bury them deeply; you can always sift a little more over them the next day if some show. This will sometimes happen when the soil has settled after watering.
5. Stand the flat in a tub of water, being careful that the water only comes about three-quarters of the way up its side. The object of this is to allow the soil to *suck up* water. Watering from above will often float the seed, and seldom penetrates to the soil at the bottom of the flat. Thus all the soil would dry out quickly.

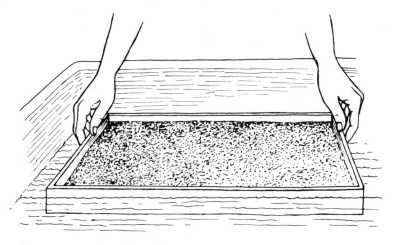

Bottom watering allows the soil to suck up the water it requires.

Note: An old sink or wash tub is very useful for this job. But be very sure when you are buying it, that it is big enough to put the seed flats in and take out, without having to tilt or maneuver them in any way.

6. When the soil has sucked up enough water to show a moist surface, lift the flat out and allow it to drain.
7. Cover the flat with a sheet of glass, then a thickly folded newspaper.
8. Turn the glass daily, so that a dry side is next to the soil.
9. If the soil shows signs of drying out, repeat the soaking (Step 5).
10. As soon as there is any sign of green showing, remove the glass, but shade the little plants which are emerging with a newspaper for a few days, gradually allowing more light and sun to reach them. Do not allow them to dry out, but beware of over-watering, too! Only experience will make you a good judge of your plants' needs. It is worth the trouble of continuing to water from below at this stage.

WHEN SMALL QUANTITIES OF ANY ONE HERB ARE NEEDED

1. Fill as many pots with soil mix as there are kinds of Herbs to be sown. Mark on each pot with a waterproof pen, the name of the Herb to be sown in that pot.
2. Tamp the soil down gently, so that it is about half an inch from the top of the pot.
3. Sow the seed, very finely, one Herb to each pot.
4. From here onward, follow directions in the previous section, substituting the word "pot" for "flat."

Note: *Never* try sowing several different kinds of Herb seeds in one container. Germination times are different, and you will not be able to give each Herb its individual needs.

EXTRA WARMTH FOR HEAT-LOVING SEEDS

Sometimes seeds require a higher temperature than that which is available in your greenhouse. It is very uneconomical to raise the temperature of your whole greenhouse just to germinate seeds, so here are two methods which can be used:

If you have a whole flat of seeds needing some heat, put a 25-watt light bulb in a wooden apple box, and rest the seed flat on top.

If you have only a few pots of seeds needing extra heat, these can be stood in a seed flat, and the whole thing placed on the apple box as above. However, if you can find the type of tin oven which used to be used over a kerosene stove or burner, this is more efficient. A 15-watt light bulb will hold the oven at a temperature of 80° to 90° F. (26° to 32° C.). This is adequate for Basil, Sweet Marjoram, and incidentally, for tomatoes and sweet peppers.

DAMPING OFF

This destructive fungus can destroy hundreds of seedlings in a matter of days, but the only Herb seedlings which we ever lost this way were Basil (all varieties), but other seedlings *can* be destroyed by it. It thrives in a damp atmosphere, so once your glass comes off the seeds, put the containers where there is good air circulation. It is more likely to appear where seedlings are too crowded. so sow seeds thinly. A light covering of clean sand or "Perlite" can be sprinkled over the soil when the seeds are sown, to absorb excess moisture.

If, with all these precautions, your little seedlings flop over, the stems seeming to give way where they emerge from the soil, they have "damped off," and there is nothing you can do about it, except set another lot of seeds to germinate.

Another precaution which can be taken to stop this fungus from destroying your seedlings is to soak the soil with *Cheshunt Compound Fungicide*. The seed pots or boxes may be stood in it, instead of in plain water, at their initial watering.

To make Cheshunt Compound Fungicide:

Take 2 parts by weight of Copper Sulphate (finely ground) and 11 parts by weight of Ammonium Carbonate (fresh). Mix together and store in an airtight *glass* jar.

When this fungicide is needed, dissolve one ounce of the mixture in a little hot water, and when it is thoroughly dissolved, make up to 2½ U.S. gallons with cold water, and use immediately. It is wise to use plastic or porcelain containers, not metal, with this liquid.

If you are still troubled by seedlings damping off, in spite of the

LAVENDER (*Lavandula officinalis*)—Dwarf
and Semi-Dwarf varieties

precautions you take, consult your local Agricultural Extension Service and remember that damping off is easier to prevent than to cure.

TRANSPLANTING

Transplanting to individual pots may be started as soon as the first "true" leaves are *just* beginning to show. (The first leaves which appear are the cotyledons and do not look in the least like the true or typical leaves of the plant.)

There is a lot of argument about the advisability of such early transplanting, but we found that it worked well for transplanting into pots, though not to the ground outside. The roots are quite tiny at this stage, and great care must be taken not to break them.

1. Fill the pots into which you are going to transplant the seedlings with a suitable mix (see Chapter 2). The size pot which we found was most useful at this stage was a *square* three-inch, and for Parsley plants a tall 2¼-inch rose pot was ideal.
2. With an old table knife or *dibber* (if you can buy a really small one) or a wooden spatula (such as a doctor's depresser), lift the little plant out of the soil. The roots will probably lose most of the soil that was on them, but this does not matter—unlike planting out from individual pots into the garden, when the soil around the roots should *not* be disturbed.
3. Make a hole in the soil of a transplanting pot, lower gently into it the roots and some of the stem, curling it around if necessary.
4. Press the soil around the stem, gently but firmly.
5. When all the seedlings are transplanted, water from below.

Your Herb plants will grow on happily until the roots start to fill the pots, and just before they reach this stage they either should be sold, planted out into the garden (see "Planting Your Herb Plants"), or potted into bigger pots.

The last is to be avoided if possible, since it is a time-consuming process. It rarely warrants doing (commercially), except in the case of a few quick-growing or large-rooted plants; and for large-sized plants for indoor culture.

A fertilizer (see Chapter 2) should be added to the water about every 10 days, and plants may be watered from above after the first bottom watering.

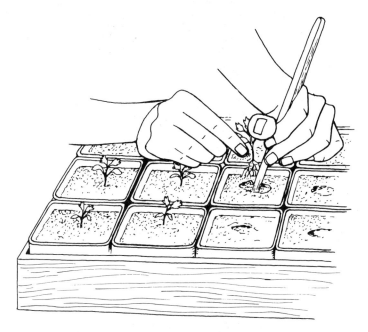

Transplanting seedlings into three-inch-square pots.

PLASTIC PLANT POTS

All through this book I have recommended using square pots. They take up less room, are quick to set into flats, and leave no room for the soil to run between them when filling. They are easy to pack for shipping, fit together compactly, and do not fall over in transit. To start you off, buy a case each of 3-inch squares, 4-inch squares, and 2¼-inch square "rose pots" (these are tall ones).

If you use secondhand pots, they must be sterilized. Consult your Agricultural Extension Service on how to use the poisonous formulin necessary to do the job. Don't use tin cans for your plants: they do nothing for them!

GARLIC (*Allium sativum*)

CHAPTER 4

A Guide To the Vegetative Propagation of Perennial Herbs

Vegetative propagation, used by gardeners to reproduce perennial plants, is an asexual method, whereas propagation by seeds is basically a sexual process.

In this chapter you will find a list of 46 perennial Herbs, showing how each one can be propagated. Following this, is a reference list of eight methods of vegetative propagation, showing which perennial Herbs can be propagated by each method, and these methods are then described in detail.

The advantages of vegetative propagation are twofold: Herb plants produced this way will reach selling and cropping size more rapidly than plants of the same Herb grown from seed. Also new plants produced vegetatively will be exact replicas of the parent plant.

Remember that all perennial Herbs *can* be propagated by one or more vegetative methods; that there are a few which *must* be propagated vegetatively (as they do not seed); and that many perennial Herbs can be propagated by seed *as well as* vegetatively.

Perennial Herbs That Cannot Be Propagated From Seed

Of all the Herbs mentioned in this book, there are only a few that cannot be propagated from seed. These are the more desirable varieties of Comfrey, Garlic, the tall varieties of named Lavender,

A REFERENCE LIST OF 46 PERENNIAL HERBS
AND HOW EACH ONE CAN BE PROPAGATED

Name of Herb	How it can be Propagated Vegetatively
Agrimony	Fleshy root cuttings
Alkanet	Fleshy root cuttings
Bay	Simple layering, stem cuttings
Bedstraw	Division, runners
Bergamot	Division, cuttings
Burnet, Salad	Division (but not recommended, grow from seed)
Catnip	Division, stem cuttings
Chamomile, English	Division, stem cuttings
Chives	Division
Comfrey	Fleshy root cuttings
Elecampane	Fleshy root cuttings
Fennel	Division (but not recommended, grow from seed)
Garlic	Bulbs (cloves)
Garlic Chives	Division
Horehound	Division
Hyssop	Division, stem cuttings
Lavender, Tall-growing varieties	Stem cuttings
Lavender, Dwarf and Semi-Dwarf	Division, stem cuttings
Lemon Balm	Division, stem cuttings
Lovage	Division
Madder	Division, runners
Marjoram, Sweet	Simple layering, division, stem cuttings
Mints, All	Stem cuttings, runners
Oregano	Division, stem cuttings
Pennyroyal	Division, runners
Pyrethrum	Division
Rose Geranium	Stem cuttings
Rosemary	Simple layering, stem cuttings
Rue	Stem cuttings
Saffron Crocus	Corms
Sage, Broad Leaf	Simple layering, stem cuttings
Sage, Narrow Leaf	Simple layering, stem cuttings
Santolina	Simple layering, stem cuttings
Savory, Winter	Simple and stool layering, division, stem cuttings
Shallots	Bulbs
Sorrel	Division (but not recommended, treat as an annual and grow from seed)
Southernwood	Stem cuttings
Sweet Cicely	Fleshy root cuttings
Tansy	Division
Tarragon, French	Division
Thyme, Garden	Stool layering, division, stem cuttings
Thyme, Lemon	Stool layering, division, stem cuttings
Thyme, Various	All by division and stem cuttings
Verbena, Lemon	Stem cuttings
Woodruff, Sweet	Division
Wormwood	Stem cuttings

A REFERENCE LIST OF EIGHT METHODS
OF VEGETATIVE PROPAGATION
(and which perennial herbs can be propagated by each method)

By "Simple" Layering

Marjoram, Sweet
Rosemary
Sage, Broad Leaf
Sage, Narrow Leaf
Santolina
Savory, Winter

By Stool or Mound Layering

Savory, Winter
Thyme, Garden
Thyme, Lemon
Thyme, various bushy

By Division

Bedstraw
Bergamot
Burnet, Salad
Catnip
Chamomile, English
Chives
Fennel (not satisfactory,
    treat as an annual)
Garlic Chives
Horehound
Hyssop
Lavenders, Dwarf
    and Semi-Dwarf varieties
Lemon Balm
Lovage
Madder
Marjoram, Sweet
Oregano
Pennyroyal
Pyrethrum
Savory, Winter
Sorrel
Tansy
Tarragon, French
Thymes, all
Woodruff, Sweet

By Corms

Saffron Crocus

By Stem Cuttings

Bay
Bergamot
Catnip
Chamomile, English
Hyssop
Lavender, tall-growing varieties
Lavender, Dwarf
    and Semi-Dwarf varieties
Lemon Balm
Marjoram, Sweet
Mints, all
Oregano
Rose Geranium
Rosemary
Rue
Sage, Broad Leaf
Sage, Narrow Leaf
Santolina
Savory, Winter
Southernwood
Thymes, all
Verbena, Lemon
Wormwood

By Fleshy Root Cuttings

Agrimony
Alkanet
Comfrey
Elecampane
Sweet Cicely

By Runners

Bedstraw
Madder
Mints, all
Pennyroyal

By Bulbs

Garlic
Shallots

most Mints, (though you are unlikely to get a really good commercial strains from seed), Southernwood, French Tarragon, and
Lemon Thyme. Shallots and Saffron Crocus *can* be grown from
seed, but they seldom are commercially.

Simple Layering

Layering is one of the simplest methods of propagating plants. Some
Herbs layer themselves naturally, putting down roots where their
decumbent stems or branches touch the soil. An advantage of
propagating by this method is that the branch or stem to be rooted
remains attached to the parent plant, until it has grown its own
roots. Thus it has a source of nourishment until you are ready to cut
if off and transplant it.

The new roots will develop more rapidly if the branch or stem is
pegged in soil which is friable, well-drained and yet capable of
holding moisture and not drying out. So if it is necessary to improve
the soil where the branches or stems are to be pegged down, add a
little sand and well-moistened peat moss a day or two before the
layering is to be done.

HOW TO DO SIMPLE LAYERING

1. Select a stem or branch of the parent Herb plant which will
   bend easily and touch the soil.
2. Make an incision just below a node, cutting at a slant *halfway
   through* the stem or branch.
                              or
   Scrape away the outer layer of bark from a short section of
   stem or branch without cutting into it. This, the better
   method for thin stems, is called "wounding" the stem.
3. Measure where the incision in the branch will touch the soil,
   and scoop away enough to form a shallow depression.
4. Peg the branch down with 8-inch (20 cm.) lengths of wire (cut
   them from a coat hanger). Don't use a shorter length, as it will
   work loose in time, and your new roots may lift out of the
   ground.
5. Fill the depression with soil, firming it well.
6. Water thoroughly.
7. Place a brick over the spot where the incision (or wound) is

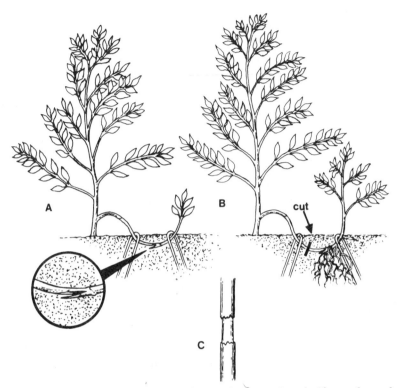

Make an incision just below a node, cutting at a slant halfway through the stem or branch. (A) Peg the branch down with eight-inch (20 cm.) lengths of wire. (B) Six to eight weeks after layering, check for root growth by moving soil away from the wound. (C) Scraping away the outer layer of bark is an alternative method to making an incision.

buried. This will help to conserve moisture as well as keep it in place.

8. Six to eight weeks after layering, check for root growth by moving soil away from the wound. The exact time it will take for roots to form depends on the time of year, the variety of Herb, and your skill as a propagator.

Layering can be started in the spring. Use the growth of the previous year. By mid-summer it will be possible to use the current year's new growth, rather than the older wood of the previous year. This new growth will be much more flexible, and is often easier to handle without breakage. Layering can be continued till four weeks before the first fall frost is expected.

The plants layered early in the year will be ready to be moved by early fall or before. But most of those layered in late summer or early fall will have to be left attached to their parent plant until spring growth starts again the following year.

Use simple layering to increase your stock plants, to produce large, "instant" pot plants (see Chapter 6, "Indoor Culture"), and plants to set out for field growing, (see Chapter 6, "Field-grown Plants"). This method is seldom suitable for producing *small* commercial plants, as the branches and stems which are suitable for layering are usually too big to fit into 3- or 4-inch square pots.

Stool or Mound Layering

There is another method of layering which is suitable for bushy perennial Herbs. It is called stool or mound layering.

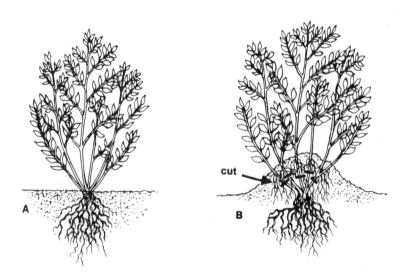

(A) A suitable type of plant for stool or mountd layering. (B) The same plant several months after it has been stool- or mound-layered, showing new root growth on buried stems.

HOW TO DO STOOL OR MOUND
LAYERING

1. Mound soil up around the center of the plant, burying the center branches completely. This is usually done in early fall to have plants ready for the following spring, but it can be done any other time of the year if you wish.
2. Take care that the branches are always covered with soil. If rains wash it away, replace it at once.
3. In late spring, dig the plants up. Roots should have formed all over the buried branches, and any pieces with a few leaves and some roots can be cut off to be replanted, either in pots or directly into the beds.

Which ever way you do layering, remember to wait until there is good root growth on the buried stems before you cut them off and plant them in their new location.

Division

Another method of propagation is by division of the whole plant and its roots. This method is used for perennial Herb plants which grow from a number of stems. It is not suitable for those which grow from one single central stem. (See "Herbs That Can Be Propagated by Division.")

HOW TO DIVIDE HERB PLANTS

1. Lift the mother plant carefully with a fork.
2. Wash the roots with a hose gun to remove all the soil. The formation of the whole plant can then be seen, making it easy to see where to divide it.
3. Depending on the type of plant formation, either pull apart the plant or cut off the younger new plant growth around the central older growth. This old growth can be discarded. The new growth will supply you with new plants.
4. Trim some of the leaves and stems off the new little plants

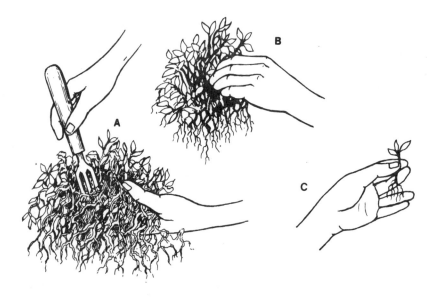

(A) Pulling a plant apart. (B) Selecting a plantlet for potting. (C) Showing plantlet after removal from parent plant.

before replanting them. This avoids excessive loss of moisture while the plant is re-establishing itself. The roots should also be trimmed, to encourage new growth.

5. Small divisions can be potted into three- and/or four-inch square pots. Larger divisions are planted into the garden to increase your stock, or to grow on for selling as "field" plants. They also can be potted into large pots to sell as "instant" pot plants (see Chapter 6, "Indoor Culture").

Division can be carried out in the spring as soon as growth is about to begin, and in early fall if plants are to be set out in the garden. If plants are to be potted and brought into the greenhouse, then division can be done up until quite late in the year—even into winter in the case of some very hardy Herbs. Much depends on your climate and your facilities. So when you have sufficient stock to be able to experiment, do so.

Remember that you must not sell these plant divisions until they have had time to settle down and get growing again in their new location—whether this is in a pot or in the field. It will take a little time for them to establish themselves after being separated from the parent plants. Do not let them dry out.

MARJORAM, SWEET (*Marjorana hortensis*)

69

MINT, ENGLISH (*Mentha cardifolia*)

Stem Cuttings

Most perennial Herbs can be started from cuttings (see "Herbs That Can Be Propagated by Stem Cuttings"). Terminal cuttings are made from the soft wood at the tip of a branch (or stem). Heel cuttings are made from the base of the branch (or stem) where it joins the main branch (or stem) of the plant. There is no reason why a center section should not also be rooted, if the growth is long enough to allow for this.

Cuttings may be taken whenever there is suitable material available. Usually by late spring or early summer the new growth is long enough. From 2 to 6 inches (5 to 15 cm.) of this new growth can be used for each cutting, shorter cuttings making more compact plants than the long ones. Remove half the leaves to check wilting caused by transpiration.

Note that if small pot plants are required for winter sales, (see Chapter 6, "Christmas Sales"), propagation by cuttings may be done in the fall. The material available at this time will be "harder" than in summer, and may take a little longer to root. These cuttings, however, will not be "hardwood" cuttings. Rooting hardwood cuttings involves a completely different technique, which is not used for any of the Herbs in this book.

Before taking your cuttings from the Herb plants in the garden, get these things ready:

1. Pruning shears to cut material from stock plants.
2. A piece of clean wood the size of a kitchen chopping board.
3. A Stanley or Exacto knife with a new, sharp blade.
4. Clean seed flats and/or clay pots.
5. Hormone rooting powder—the mildest strength marked "for softwood cuttings."
6. Large plastic bags and wet newspapers.
7. Sterile material in which to root the cuttings. This may be clean, washed sand, perlite, powdered styrofoam, vermiculite, or a mixture of sand and one of the others in equal proportions. Peat moss is not recommended, since it tends to get soggy. Everybody finds his favorite medium, by trial and error. Personally, I liked a mixture of sand and perlite. Whatever you do use, do not pack it tightly round the stems. It isn't necessary, and makes removal of the rooted cutting difficult to do without damaging it.

All this ready? Now:

1. Fill flats or pots with rooting medium, and water it.
2. Cut material from stock plants in the garden with pruning shears or Stanley knife.
3. Put this cut material between wet newspapers or in a plastic bag, being sure the bag is large enough not to damage the stems or leaves. Then, working in the lath house or potting shed,
4. Put a small amount of plant material on the cutting board, and using the sharp Stanley knife, cut pieces of stem off just below a node. Some people insist that the cut must be at an angle, others that it should be at right angles to the stem. I found little difference in results, whichever way I cut. Try to keep the cuttings between 2 and 6 inches (5 to 15 cm.) in

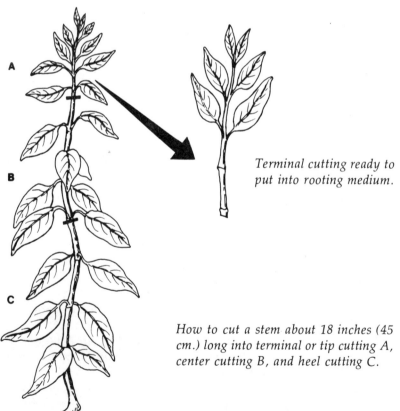

Terminal cutting ready to put into rooting medium.

How to cut a stem about 18 inches (45 cm.) long into terminal or tip cutting A, center cutting B, and heel cutting C.

Insert the cuttings about half their length into the rooting medium, at an angle of about 45 degrees.

length. You may find you can make three from one stem: a tip, a center, and a heel cutting. (See illustration, p. 72).

5. Strip at least half of the leaves off of each cutting.
6. Put each cutting in a plastic bag till you are ready to put it in the rooting medium. Do not prepare more than 50 cuttings before going on to the next step. (There is no reason why cuttings of different varieties of Herbs should not be put in the same flat or pot. But label them carefully with name of Herb and date when the cutting was taken. Use plastic or wooden labels, writing on them with a garden pencil or *waterproof* felt pen.)
7. Dip the cut end of the cutting into the hormone rooting powder. (This step is optional—there is much controversy about the necessity of it.)
8. Gently tap off *surplus* rooting powder.
9. Insert the cuttings about half their length into the rooting medium, angled at about 45 degrees.
10. Repeat steps 7, 8, and 9 until the flat is filled with cuttings— about one square inch (2½ square cm.) apart.
11. Give the cuttings some shade for at least a week, then plenty of light but no direct sunlight. Water them frequently.
12. To see if rooting has started, pull gently on a cutting. If some resistance is felt, the roots are forming. But if you are using sand alone as a rooting medium, do *not* pull. The sand holds so firmly, especially when wet, that there will be resistance whether the roots have formed or not. It will be necessary to lift a cutting out of the sand with a plant ladle or dibber, to check on root growth.

*Transplant the cuttings into the soil
when the roots are about an inch
long (2½ cm.).*

13. Transplant the cuttings into soil when the roots are about an
    inch (2½ cm.) long. There will be little, if any, new top
    growth at this stage.
14. Give the newly transplanted cuttings shade for a few days.

Although it is true that roots will grow from some Herb cuttings if
they are put in a glass of water, this method is not recommended,
since the roots formed are usually very brittle. This method is not
recommended for rooting commercial quantities of cuttings.

There are several things which can be done to improve on this
very basic and simple method of rooting cuttings. Polyethylene can
be used to cover the whole flat to conserve the moisture. Plastic bags
can be used to cover pots in the same way, and for the same
purpose. One of the difficulties which may arise when this method
is used, is the appearance of various fungi diseases, which thrive in
excessive moisture.

Better than polyethylene is a cover of glass, so that ventilation can
be controlled more easily. An old aquarium can be used, but gives
inadequate room when large quantities of cuttings are being
rooted.

If you are likely to go into large-scale production of plants by
cuttings, you should look into the cost of setting up mist propagation. It is a comparatively new technique, but well proven. A
constant or intermittent mist is maintained over the cuttings; this
can be controlled manually or by a timing device. This mist pre-
vents loss by wilting and drying out, and it also tends to speed up
the formation of roots.

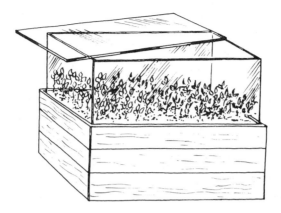

A home-made propagating case. Bottom heat may be supplied by a 25-watt light bulb in the wooden box.

Bottom heat may also be applied with electric heating cables to accelerate rooting. If you have no greenhouse, a cold frame with a heating cable would be an invaluable aid. A temperature of 65° to 70° F. (18° to 21° C.) is adequate. In the greenhouse an arrangement with a light bulb is often sufficient to supply this amount of heat.

Remember that all plants must be well rooted, and then grown on till they become sturdy and well leaved, before they are sold. Never sell rooted cuttings. It doesn't pay. By potting them and holding them a few weeks, you will have well-grown plants with very little more work or cost.

Root Cuttings

A few fleshy, thick-rooted Herbs sprout several shoots from the top of their roots. Propagation is carried out by slicing the root in pieces, so that each piece has some of the fleshy root and a bud. The pieces are then buried just below the surface of the soil, either in a pot or the ground, and kept well watered.

The best time to propagate by this method is in the spring, as soon as new growth starts, though with care it can be done at almost any time from early spring to fall, as long as the newly planted roots can be kept shaded and moist. If leaf growth has become heavy, remove most of it before replanting, leaving only a small center leaf, and plant so that it is above the soil and the piece of the root is below.

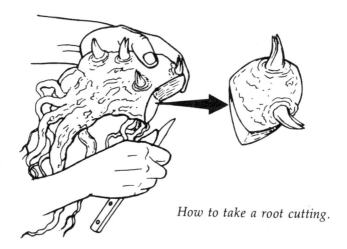

How to take a root cutting.

New, small roots will grow from the pieces of the old root, and when the growth of the leaves is well started, the plant is ready to sell or plant out.

Runners

A runner is a trailing stem which will take root at the nodes. Sometimes the stem travels over the ground and sometimes under it. To propagate from either type requires the same technique. It is best done in spring, when growth is just beginning, or after the final harvest is cut in early fall.

To prepare the material for planting as small pot plants:

1. Sever 2-inch (5 cm.) pieces of root, with at least one node on each one.
2. Replant 1 inch (2½ cm.) below the soil, three pieces to a 4-inch square pot.
3. Water.

To prepare material for planting in beds:

1. Sever 6-inch (15 cm.) pieces of root, with several nodes on each.
2. Replant six to eight pieces per square foot (30 sq. cm.) of bed, depending on material available.

CORIANDER (*Coriandrum sativum*)

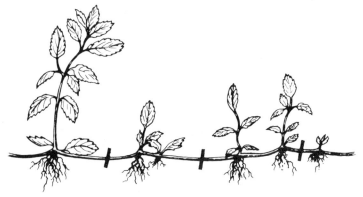

Sever two-inch (5 cm.) pieces of root, with at least one node on each piece.

Bulbs or Cloves

Shallots and Garlic are the two Herbs propagated by bulbs.

Shallots are planted one by one, and during the season will divide themselves, until by the late summer there are little "nests," with 8 to 12 new bulbs where you planted one. Each one of these new bulbs may be planted for next year's crop—an increase of from 800 to 1200 percent!

Garlic forms a cluster of cloves, and these have to be separated carefully, and each one planted. They in their turn will form a cluster, giving you a large increase. (See Chapter 3, List E, for details of culture of both these Herbs.)

A cluster of Shallot bulbs.

How to prepare Garlic for planting.

Corms

The Saffron Crocus is propagated by corms, which in turn form *cormlets* round the base of the old bulb, and each cormlet can be re-planted. (See Chapter 9, "More Herbs to Grow," for details of culture.)

Remember that this chapter is intended to give you a guide to the vegetative propagation of all the Herbs mentioned in this book. The way to become proficient is to practice all these methods, to study the forms of growth of the Herb plants, and to read as many practical, well-illustrated books as you can about propagation.

Recommended Reading

Handbook on Propagation, No. 24. Brooklyn Botanic Garden, 100 Washington Avenue, Brooklyn, New York 11225.

Plant Propagation in Pictures, by Montague Free. American Garden Guild, Inc. and Doubleday & Co., Inc., Garden City, New York.

OREGANO (*Origanum vulgare*)

CHAPTER 5

Harvesting, Drying, Storing and Freezing Herbs

How and When to Harvest

The time to harvest Herbs whose leaves are to be dried is when their volatile oil content is at its highest. Ideally, harvesting should be done between the time the flower buds first appear and before they are fully open. If harvested earlier, the oil content has not fully developed, and so the flavor will not be fully developed either. If harvested any later the oil content will have diminished.

The time of day when you harvest is important. Try to do it early in the morning before the sun gets hot, but after it has had time to dry the dew on the leaves. If you can, the day before you cut any leafy Herbs, hose them over with a gentle spray to wash off any dirt and dust. By doing it the day before, there will be time for them to dry off before you cut them.

Leafy *annual* Herbs can be cut back to leave only four inches of stem. They will then grow again, and give you one or two more cuts later in the year. Cutting should be done with pruning shears or a Stanley knife. Do not *pick* the stems off—you may pull too hard and damage the roots, or even pull the plants right out of the soil. Remember that annual Herb plants, from which you want to harvest seed, should not be cut back for their leaves.

Leafy *perennial* Herbs should not be cut back as severely as the annual ones. Only one-third of their growth should be removed for drying, and in some cases only the leafy tips (see chart: "Part of Herb to be Harvested"). Remember that when you are harvesting bushy perennials you are also pruning them; cut them carefully so that they will produce new growth and keep their compact shape. Do not cut too drastically in the first few years of a perennial Herb's life! Most perennial Herbs will be ready for cutting before or during July, and you will probably get another cut in September. In mild climates you may even get three cuts.

Many perennials have tough branches and stems, and in this case use pruning shears. Softer stems may be cut with a Stanley knife. Be sure your cutting tools are sharp, for even more care is needed than with the annual Herbs not to damage the roots. Never pull or break off branches or stems.

Do not pile up the fresh-cut Herbs or put them in a sack. They will heat up and get crushed, causing loss of the volatile oils. Put them loosely in *shallow* boxes. If you have hosed them over the day before cutting, as advised above, you will not have the fiddly job of washing all the little pieces of the plant which you have cut.

The harvest should be taken to your drying facilities as quickly as possible, and drying started at once. Don't leave the Herbs lying about, and remember not to cut more than your drying facilities can handle at one time.

There is no point in stripping the leaves off the stems before drying them. I have often seen this suggested, but I cannot see the point; it takes much longer to do than when they are dry, and the leaves get bruised when handled—with a resulting loss of essential oils. To dry stripped leaves, except by the oven method, would also be a problem, since the air currents would blow them all over the drying room.

If flowers are to be harvested, they should be fully open when picked for drying.

When seeds are needed, these should be collected when the heads (containing the seeds) are turning brown. A close watch has to be kept on the plants to catch them at the right moment—which is before the seeds start to fall, but not until they are beginning to ripen. If the plant is tapped or shaken gently and a few seeds fall, it is time to cut off the heads. Cut them into a paper bag to carry to your drying area.

When roots of the Herbs are needed, they are dug as soon as the leaves of the plant have begun to die down, which is usually in the late fall. Dig with a garden fork, being very careful not to damage them. Clean them with a hose gun, but do not use a brush, for the bristles may damage them.

ALKANET (*Alkanna tinctoria*)

How to Dry Herbs

Many people are under the impression that all Herbs *must* be dried before use, but this is not so. Most Herbs can be used fresh *or* dried, and the only one I know which *has* to be dried before use is Sweet Woodruff—it has no smell when fresh. Chives are much better used fresh—no way of processing (even freeze-drying) has been found which retains all of their flavor.

The method you employ for drying depends mainly on the quantities you have to handle. Small amounts of leafy Herbs can be dried in an airy room—preferably in the dark, but definitely in the absence of sunlight. The humidity must be low. Tied in small bunches and hung upside down, most of them will dry in about two weeks in warm summer weather. The exception to this is curly Parsley, which needs some artificial heat to dry quickly enough to retain its flavor and a good color. (For full details, see "Drying the Parsley" in Chapter 7.)

For quick-drying of small quantities of the leafy Herbs, the slow oven method is excellent. It will not damage the color or flavor as long as the temperature is held between 95° F. (35° C.) and 77° F. (25° C.). Hotter than the maximum will dry out the oils and damage the flavor and color. Cooler than the suggested minimum will slow up the drying process, and could cause condensation which might result in an off-flavor, caused by mold.

Some electric ovens can be held under 95° F., and the *warming* oven on oil, wood or coal stoves often is adequate, though the temperature is hard to keep steady for any length of time. Best to use is a gas oven in which a pilot light is always burning; a steady temperature of about 90° F. (32° C.) is easy to maintain. Check with a thermometer and adjust the strength of the tiny gas jet if necessary. Drying by this cool oven method will take from 24 to 48 hours, depending on the Herb being dried, and the steadiness of the temperature.

Some people insist that drying with any artificial heat causes loss of flavor and color, but providing that the temperatures are kept within the suggested limits above, this is not so. Personally, I found that the cool oven method produced a far superior product to the "natural" drying, which depends too much on uncontrolled conditions. High humidity is particularly damaging.

To dry larger quantities of Herbs, you will need to equip a room or shed with a steady flow of warm air, and a means of exhausting the moist air. The most economical way to do this is with a fan with a heating element and an extractor fan. The Herbs can be hung upside down in bunches, or can be spread on drying trays which have bottoms made of cheesecloth or nylon net. These trays are slid into racks, which should be made with wheels or castors so that they can be moved about easily.

Flowers to be dried should be spread out on drying trays, and they can be dried in either of the above ways. It would be wise to keep the temperature well below the suggested maximum of 95° F. (35° C.) and when drying by the oven method not above 80° F. (30° C.).

Herbs which you grow for their seeds, if harvested as suggested earlier in this Chapter, will need further drying. Spread out the seed heads on papers on the floor or on Herb-drying trays and put them in a dry, airy location. Don't use a fan—you'll blow away the seeds! Leave the heads for a few days, until the seeds are dry enough to be shaken out of their pods. Small seeds can be rubbed out, but be gentle and do not bruise them. Then dry them for a few more days before putting them into airtight containers. Inspect the containers regularly every few days for several weeks, to check for any sign of dampness. If there is any sign of dampness thoroughly re-dry the seeds and containers.

Some artificial heat is usually needed to dry the roots of Herbs. By the time the roots are dug for drying, in the fall, the weather is not likely to be warm or dry enough to do the job outside. Either the oven method, as described for drying leaves, or a drying room with warm air circulating from a fan, should be used. Large roots should be sliced about one quarter-inch thick. They will take from three to five weeks (possibly more) to dry, depending on their condition and the drying temperatures. To be ready to store, they must break with a snap when bent over. Store them in airtight containers.

How to Prepare and Store
Dried Herbs

Opinions differ a little as to the correct time to rub down your leafy Herbs for storing. Some people advise drying them until the stems, as well as the leaves, crackle when touched—but some Herb leaves

FENNEL (*Foeniculum vulgare*)

would be over-dry by this time. So rub the leaves off the stems when *they* are crackly. Then, if the stems are to be used, too, they should be subjected to more drying until they too are crackly and can be broken down easily.

It is not often that culinary Herb stems are used. There are a few exceptions, which will be noted in the list giving parts of the Herb to dry, and manufacturers packing medicinal Herbs sometimes use them.

If you are processing culinary Herbs for your own sales, the most practical way to powder them is to use a blender. If you want a "flaky" product, hand rubbing will achieve this.

If you are processing the leaves of Herbs for teas, they should be kept as whole as possible, so very careful handling is necessary to produce an attractive and well-flavored product. Remember that your object is to produce dried Herbs which are green and full-flavored.

In all cases, except where you are selling direct to the public (when the preceding directions should help you), discuss with your buyers the form in which they prefer to receive their dried Herbs, and try to cater for each one's needs—Herbs for dyers being a case in point.

No dried Herbs should be kept more than a year, if you want to be sure of keeping up top-quality flavor, even though some of them may *seem* to be as good as they were when first dried. There is a theory that powdered Herbs lose their flavor faster than those left whole, though I have never found this to be so as long as they are kept in airtight containers in the dark.

The question of containers for storage and selling is important. For storage, large glass bottles are best, one advantage being that during the first few weeks after storing it is easy to see if any moisture appears, indicating inadequate drying. If this happens, the Herbs must be re-dried. The Herbs should be kept in a dark cupboard, unless you are able to get dark-colored bottles. You may also store them in plastic bags or tins. Whatever containers you use, they must be *absolutely* airtight. Be sure they are clean and completely dry before the Herbs are put in.

If you are selling wholesale, your buyers may have some preference as to the type of containers you should use. Consult them. For retail sales, there are many different types of containers available— from small plastic or cellophane bags, through all shapes and sizes of glass bottles to beautiful ceramic containers. You may find a market for any or all of these.

SAGE (*Salvia officinalis*)—Narrow leaf

How to Freeze Herbs

Herbs to be frozen should be harvested at the same time and in the same way as Herbs which are to be dried. All the equipment you need is pint and pint-and-a-half plastic freezer bags, labels, and "twistems."

Culinary Herb leaves which retain their flavor well when frozen are: Basils (though they discolor badly), Chervil, Dill, Lemon Balm, Lovage, Sweet Marjoram, all the Mints, Oregano, Parsley, Rosemary, Sages, Savories, French Tarragon, Garden and Lemon Thymes, and Lemon Verbena.

Chervil, Dill, Sweet Marjoram, Rosemary, the Savories, Tarragon and Thymes can be frozen on their stems. Snip the other Herb leaves off the stems. Package them carefully, without crowding them in the bags, label with the name of the Herb and the date of freezing, and close the bag with a "twistem." Place them in the freezer where they will not be crushed by heavier packages. It is *not* necessary to blanch them before freezing.

Garlic and Shallots should be peeled and chopped before freezing. Enclose in two sealed bags to prevent odor escaping into the freezer!

Frozen Herbs retain their flavor for a very long time. I have had Marjoram in a home freezer for three years, and to me it tasted as good as the day it was put in. I do not, of course, recommend keeping a commercial product frozen for this length of time, but I mention it to show you how well some Herbs do retain their flavor when frozen.

The markets in which to sell frozen Herbs are limited for a small grower. Try selling them directly from your farm, packaged in the plastic bags (1 pint and 1½ pints). If you can get smaller sizes, and have the patience, make up single servings of individual Herbs also. Price frozen Herbs a little higher than you would similiar quantities of the fresh ones, to cover your time and packaging costs.

Remember that you need as much of the frozen Herb as you do the fresh Herb, to obtain the same amount of flavor.

SAVORY, SUMMER (*Satureia hortensis*)

CHAPTER 6

Markets and Marketing

Fresh Herbs

QUICK CASH TURNOVER

For a quick cash turnover, Parsley is hard to beat, since there is an almost limitless demand for good quality *curly* Parsley. Chefs love it for garnishing dishes, even more than for its flavor.

Chapter 7, Growing Parsley, will tell you all you need to know to get into this paying crop. Details for growing all the other Herbs mentioned in this section, will be found by referring to the index of 32 Basic Herbs in Chapter 3.

Another quick cash crop is Dill, for selling at cucumber-pickling time. The stems and foliage are all that is required—not the seeds— for the growing and threshing of seeds is not an economical commercial proposition for the small grower. A market should be lined up in advance, preferably before the seed is even sown. Large produce stores, supermarkets, or wholesale produce suppliers are all possible outlets for your crop.

The seed is planted in late spring and cropped in late summer. The time to harvest the Dill is before the seeds start to form, and while the crop is still green. It is cut off at ground level, and about six stems are bunched together, and then these are made into bundles of twelve bunches.

A word of warning: Dill is the only Herb which I have ever seen badly infested with aphids, and if they attack your crop it is a total loss, and has to be burned. The only preventitive is a toxic spray, and as we wouldn't spray, regretfully we dropped field-growing Dill.

Chervil is another annual Herb which grows quickly from a fall or early spring planting, and like Parsley it is cut and bunched. The demand is limited, but continental chefs really appreciate it. It does not retain a good flavor when dried.

There may be a small demand for fresh Sweet Basil foliage. Small bunches of eight to ten stems should be made up and stood in water (like Parsley). Do not refrigerate it, as the leaves may turn brown.

There also may be a small demand for Coriander and Caraway seed. Coriander is an annual, while Caraway is a biennial. A bigger outlet for these two seeds is more likely to be found in the dried Herb markets.

NOT QUITE SO QUICK, BUT PROFITABLE

Under this heading come Garlic and Shallots.

Garlic can be planted a week or two before your first expected frost in fall. This allows rooting to take place, but green top growth is unlikely to appear until the following spring. Where winters are severe, however, this may result in loss of the cloves. If this happens, plant new cloves as early in the spring as you can work the soil. Both plantings will mature in late summer, but the fall-planted crop will give the heaviest yield.

Shallots should be sown in very late fall, about a month later than Garlic, if the ground is still unfrozen. Otherwise plant them as early in the spring as possible.

Both the Garlic cloves and Shallot bulbs should be bought from a reliable source, since both of them can be troublesome if grown from inferior stock. They are marketed by weight. When packaging, never use plastic or cellophane containers, since both of these Herbs need to breathe.

If you find that either of these two Herbs grows well in your garden, try to find a market before you go into growing it heavily. Shallots may be more difficult to sell, since they are not appreciated by everybody. I remember an angry restaurant owner, who complained about the price of the "fancy onions" we had sold to his chef!

Suggestions for growing Garlic and Shallots will be found in Chapter 3, List E.

LONG-TERM, LONG-LASTING
PERENNIAL MONEY-MAKERS

Without doubt, fresh Chives are the biggest money maker in this group. Chefs appreciate them, because there is *no* substitute for the fresh Chives. Freeze-dried they give a "little bit of color," but little flavor.

It may be 12 months from the time you sow the seed, in early spring, till you can take the first worthwhile commercial crop from the plants. But if you can buy plants, you will get a crop almost immediately.

Chives are a lot of work. The planting, growing, watering, weeding, cutting, cleaning and packaging have to be done regularly. Foresight and planning are also needed to ensure that you will have enough to keep up regular supplies. But they *do* pay a good return for all this work. In Chapter 7 you will find all you need to know to grow and market them.

Many chefs will want fresh French Tarragon, too. It will take you several years to build up your stock plants, so don't start deliveries until you are sure you can keep up supplies. Meanwhile, make Tarragon vinegar (See Chapter 10, "Culinary Products to Make With Fresh Herbs") with your surplus; there is a ready market for it in gourmet shops and health food stores.

Other fresh perennial Herbs which you may be asked to supply are Sweet Marjoram, Mint (English), Rosemary, Sage, Summer Savory, and Garden Thyme.

All the fresh Herbs you supply should be handled by you personally without a middleman. Then you can be sure that the quality is not impaired by somebody refrigerating them, or not delivering them the same day. You will also get the retail price for them, and last but by no means least, it's great fun getting to know the chefs, and going behind the scenes in hotels and restaurants. When making deliveries, be sure to be clean and tidy in your appearance.

Other outlets for fresh Herbs should be searched for. Natural food stores may like to market bunches of fresh Herbs, though unless you are very near to these stores, you may not find the deliveries worthwhile. They will certainly want deliveries made more often than once a week, and remember, you will only be getting wholesale prices.

Talk to produce managers in supermarkets and large stores, but

COMFREY (*Symphytum peregrinum*)

realize the same disadvantages of price and deliveries will apply in this market area too.

Do not make rash promises you cannot keep, or which will entail a lot of work for little return—unless they will give you publicity (if you want it). We were once asked by the food and drink manager of a very large hotel to grow (and pick and deliver, of course) Borage flowers to float in drinks. *Not* a paying proposition!

HERBS FOR DYEING

Color can be extracted from many plants and Herbs, usually by boiling some part or parts of them in water. This solution can then be used to dye wool, and sometimes silk and cotton also. You will find a list of Herbs for dyeing in Chapter 9.

If there is a group of weavers near you, see if they would be interested in your growing for them. You can grow, package, and dry specified Herbs according to their needs.

FLAVORING HERBS FOR
CULINARY PRODUCTS

1. Herb-flavored vinegars and oils can be made from the fresh or dried leaves of Basil, Burnet, Dill, Fennel, Garlic, Lovage, Sweet Marjoram, English Mint, Rosemary, Sage, Summer Savory, Shallots, Tarragon, and Garden Thyme.
2. Herb-flavored salad dressings may then be made from these oils and vinegars, and Herb-flavored mayonnaise also.
3. Herb-flavored jellies can be made using the fresh or dried leaves of Lemon Balm, Sweet Marjoram, many Mints, Rose Geranium, Rosemary, Sage, Summer Savory, Garden and Lemon Thymes, and Lemon Verbena.
4. Angelica stems, Borage flowers, and Mint leaves can be candied or crystalized, as can Lovage, Angelica and Sweet Cicely roots.
5. Sugar candy can be flavored with Peppermint, English Mint, Horehound, and Anise.

Directions for making all these products will be found in Chapter 10, under "Culinary Products To Make With Fresh Herbs."

COSMETIC AND PERFUME HERBS
FOR ATTRACTIVE GIFTS

1. Herbal wreaths can be made from Winter Savory, Thyme, and
   Rosemary.
2. "Tussie Mussies," which are tight little nosegays, can be
   made from many different Herbs. Directions for making them
   will be found in Chapter 10 under "Perfumed Products to
   Make With Fresh Herbs."
3. Cosmetics can be made at home using Angelica, Basil,
   Chamomile flowers, Lavender, Lemon Balm, Lemon Verbena, Lovage, most Mints (including Pennyroyal), Rosemary,
   Sage, and many of the Thymes.

Ann Tucker's *Potpourri, Incense and Other Fragrant Concoctions,*
and Beverly Plummer's *Fragrance—How to Make Unusual Soaps,
Scents and Sundries* give many good recipes. *Herbs for Health and
Cookery,* by Claire Lowenfeld and Phillipa Back has sections on
cosmetic Herbs (see Appendix D for details).

ABOUT ESSENTIAL OILS

If you are tempted to try distilling the essential oils from your
Herbs, check with local authorities first, since the laws about any
kind if distilling are very strict. Don't land yourself in jail!

You will need vast amounts of any one Herb to supply this
market, and a large acreage for growing. So it is not a field for
beginners.

Herb Plants

GROWING HERB PLANTS FOR SALE

To grow Herb plants for sale, you will need a lath house for shade in
summer, a greenhouse (unless your springs are mild and almost
frost free), a source of good Herb seeds (Appendix E), and well-
grown stock plants from which to obtain material for propagating.

"How to Start Herb Plants from Seed Indoors," in Chapter 3,

gives the information you need to grow Herbs from seeds, and Chapter 4 is your guide to vegetative propagation. In Appendix B you will find a guide to what pot sizes each Herb should be grown in, and the method of vegetative propagation to use to reproduce plants most quickly.

It is surprising how much propagating material is available from a single two- or three-year-old perennial Herb plant. For instance, a two-year-old plant of Lemon Thyme can be dug up, torn apart into many pieces, and every piece of stem which has little roots on it can be potted directly into a three- or four-inch pot, and sold after a few weeks. Other stems which have no roots can be trimmed and used to make cuttings. From a three-year-old plant of Garden Thyme as many as a hundred cuttings can be taken, though after they are rooted they will take several months to reach selling size.

Avoid repotting plants whenever you can; it is a time-consuming job, so pot all rooted plant material directly into the pot in which it is to be sold. (See chart in Appendix B.) Write the name of the Herb on each pot with a *waterproof* felt pen—it is better than using plant labels, which sometimes fall out, and is cheaper.

Pricing Herb plants for sale should not be difficult if you compare retail prices in local garden shops, and the prices of other retail sellers of Herb plants. Send for the catalogs of the three or four Herb farms which are situated nearest to you, and see what their prices are. In Appendix E you will find addresses of many Herb plant sellers, their catalog price (most growers make a small charge for them), and many other details. With several catalogs in hand to guide you, and knowledge of local retail prices, you should be able to set your retail prices. Note that your wholesale prices should be about 40–50 percent less than your retail ones.

Quality. Set and keep a high standard for quality plants. Never sell those which have grown too big for their pots, and have become rootbound. If you haven't been able to repot them before they are rootbound, they should be thrown on the compost heap. Never sell plants that look undersized; grow them on a little longer. Never sell plants whose foliage is discolored; trim it off. Never sell plants that are leggy or overgrown; most can be cut back and allowed to grow bushy before selling. In short, never sell plants in less than perfect condition. You will quickly get a good name for high quality and honesty. It is a nice reputation to have—and it pays off in every way.

SELLING HERB PLANTS RETAIL

If you decide to sell your own plants you will have to:

1. Let the public know. An attractive sign outside your place with your farm's name and indication that you sell Herb plants, is one of the best ways to get known, especially if you are situated on a well-travelled road. If your farm lies off such a road, arrange to put a sign at a nearby intersection. Keep the wording brief, and do make the lettering large enough to be read easily by passing motorists.
2. Meet the public, and find time for them whenever they stop at your farm. One of you should do the retailing, and allow the other one to get on with the work in the garden. You cannot afford the time for both of you to meet the public.
3. Establish a selling area away from the working garden and greenhouse. If possible, a second small lath house or protective structure should be built in which to keep the plants ready for sale. Those that are *not* ready for sale should be kept apart.
4. Lay out a formal Herb Garden, so that people can walk round it (without stepping on the beds). It should contain as many varieties of Herbs as possible (see Chapters 3 and 9 for suggestions), and all the plants should be labelled carefully. You will be surprised how few people know what the fully grown plants look like. This garden is a great sales stimulant.

SELLING HERB PLANTS WHOLESALE

Here again you will need a greenhouse and a lath house, but you will *not* have to meet the public or lay out your garden for show. However, you will have to find suitable sales outlets, which themselves must have:

1. A place to "hold" the plants in good condition, plenty of air and light, but not too much sun.
2. Somebody who understands about watering, and how to keep the plants healthy.
3. Somebody who knows a little about Herbs in general.

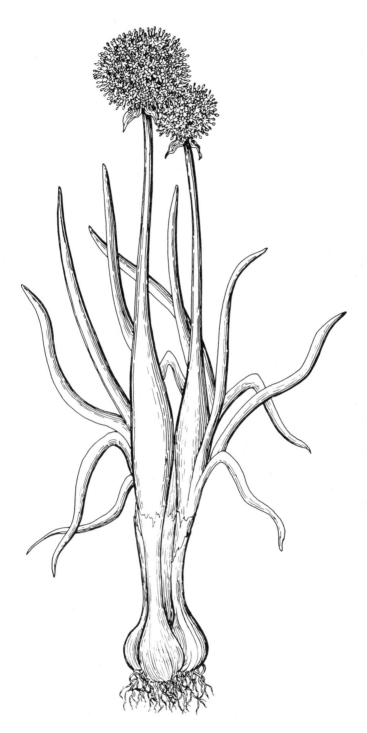

SHALLOTS (*Allium ascalonicum*)

I would suggest trying:

1. Plant and garden stores, roadside farm markets and commercial greenhouses where there is some outdoor location for the plants.
2. Natural food stores, where they can put the plants outside in an attractive and favorable setting.
3. Any store run by an owner who has an interest in Herb gardening—even if the store is not related to Herbs.

To start with, you may have to allow the retailer to have the plants on consignment, until he sees how they are going to sell. But do not continue with this arrangement for more than a few weeks. Change to a normal, outright sale at wholesale prices as quickly as possible. In larger stores the Herbs are less likely to be so well looked after if they are held on consignment. However, I have found that the small store owner will be meticulous about your property, and care for the stock as well as when he has bought it outright.

Always keep your wholesale price the same to all your retailers. It's up to them what they sell them for, though helpful suggestions from you will probably be welcome.

HALF-AND-HALF SELLING

There is a third way to sell plants which might be called "half retail–half wholesale." Arrange with a natural food store for you to spend certain afternoons or days with them, and take along plants for sale. Make arrangements to pay a flat rate for the use of the space or a percentage on sales you make there. You will soon get known as the "Herb person," but be warned that you will have to answer questions all the way from what is good for the baby's colic to how to grow psychedelic mushrooms!

ROADSIDE STANDS

Then, too, there is the roadside stand. Personally, I do not think that Herb plants *alone* warrant the work of running a stand. If you have access to somebody else's stand, which has a full range of fruits and vegetables, that would certainly be worth trying.

MAIL ORDER

Selling plants by mail order is worth considering, especially if your location is not good for selling retail, or if you do not want to deal directly with the public. You should check first with local authorities for any interstate or international regulations or restrictions on the sale of plants.

There are several ways to send plants. *Parcel post* (special handling) is one, though an extra fee over and above normal parcel postage rates is charged for this. Others include *airmail parcel post, bus, air freight,* and *United Parcel Service.*

Whichever means you use, plants must be packed with great care. After much trial and error, we found that boxes which had been used to ship liquor and wines were most suitable for packaging, since they are very strong, and plants can be slipped carefully into their individual sections. Being tall, the boxes provide protection for the foliage, too.

Cartons should be secured with twine and labelled "This side up" and "Plants, Handle with Care." Labels of this description can usually be obtained from a florist supplies wholesale outlet.

If you decide to sell by mail order, your own attractive labels should also be in a prominent place on the boxes.

It would be advisable to have a few years experience growing Herb plants before you attempt to ship them. Then you will be able to advise your customers which varieties will stand up under shipping conditions, and the best time of year to have them travel. Usually it is unwise to ship them between the first heavy frost of fall, and a month before the last frost of spring is expected.

INDOOR CULTURE

Most people who want to grow their Herb plants indoors will be satisfied to take your three- or four-inch pots of plants. They will then re-pot them themselves—as and when necessary. However, there may be a limited market for larger plants, for those people who want to be able to cut fresh Herbs from their plants at once.

To supply this market, you will have to re-pot plants from three- and four-inch pots into larger pots, and let the plants grow on for some four to eight weeks more. Use some large clay pots as well as plastic ones—some people prefer them for indoor growing.

The prices of these plants will have to be considerably higher, to compensate for the extra work, and the extra time the plants have taken up space in your greenhouse or lath house. Feel out this market carefully before plunging heavily into it, because if you do not sell the plants, you will have wasted time and space.

You will often be asked about growing plants indoors. I do not know why, but there seems to be a general misconception that Herbs will grow indoors without any special care. They need the same care as any other plants grown under artificial conditions (indoor growing is *not* natural).

A window where there is plenty of light yet not too much sun, will sometimes give fair results, but far better is to have fluorescent tubes (there are several made especially for plant-growing), which should be placed 12 to 18 inches (30 to 45 cm.) above the plants, and timed to give about 14 hours of light in the 24. In the next section are listed the Herbs which adapt themselves better than most to indoor conditions.

CHRISTMAS SALES

You will probably find that the greatest demand for Herbs to grow indoors will come around Christmas time.

You should grow them in a cool greenhouse, and below are suggested dates to give you salable plants in time for Christmas. Unless otherwise indicated, use three-inch square pots, but if you want bigger plants in larger pots, the dates will have to be put forward by four to six weeks. Pinch back all your pot plants to make them bushy.

In the late summer or early fall you will find self-sown seedlings growing around many of your Herbs in the garden. These can be dug carefully, disturbing the roots as little as possible, and potted up. Some one- and two-year-old bushy perennial Herbs can be lifted and divided, to give you salable plants quite quickly. Experiment, and keep an accurate record of dates for future reference.

Remember the speed of growth of the plants will depend on climatic and greenhouse conditions. If your plants grow more quickly than expected, they should be re-potted before they become rootbound.

Chervil. Plant seed in early October, a few seeds to a three-inch-square pot; thin out to one or two plants by nipping off the surplus seedling at the base. Do not pull them out, since that will disturb the remaining roots.

SWEET CICELY (*Myrrhis odorata*)

Chives. Dig a few plants, divide them, and pot up in four-inch-square pots in early November. See Chapter 7, "Preparing Chives for Sale as Plants."

Dill. Plant seed in mid October and handle exactly as Chervil.

Garlic Chives. Dig in late October and pot as for Chives.

Sweet Marjoram. Sow at a temperature of 80° F. (26° C.) in early September. Pot three seedlings to a three-inch square pot and keep it in the warmest part of the greenhouse. Cuttings from established plants also may be taken and potted at this time.

Mints. They are not really indoor Herbs but people do ask for them. Dig some roots in late October, and cut into three-inch lengths. Pot three pieces to a four-inch square pot.

Parsley. Parsley for Christmas needs to be sown in early August. Pot seedling up while still very small, using a "dwarf" variety and three-inch-square pots. See Chapter 6, "How to Start Parsley From Seed."

Rosemary. Probably the best Herb for Christmas sales, Rosemary, will also do better indoors than most. It is worth having several different sizes of plants. A good Rosemary for indoors is the prostrate variety, (a tender perennial that will not stand *any* frost) but it may be difficult to find stock plants. Take cuttings of all Rosemarys every month from June onwards, and you will have a variety of sizes ready for Christmas sales.

Sage. It can be propagated from cuttings early in September to give four-inch-square pot plants for Christmas. Try some in early October, too, in three-inch-square pots, and see which size sells best.

Winter Savory. Dig a plant in late October and pull it apart, planting the little rooted pieces in three-inch-square pots; or take cuttings in September.

Tarragon. I doubt that you will have any Tarragon plants to spare for winter sales. I have never tried them in the house, though they do well in the greenhouse. You would have to lift early in

October, and pot the small pieces of root, which have a shoot attached, into four-inch-square pots. This is not a good time to lift the Herb and personally I would not attempt it. To take risks with Tarragon is foolish—it's too valuable.

Thyme, Garden. In early September the plants can be dug, and rooted pieces can be potted up in three-inch-square pots. Cuttings for winter sales would have to be taken about May, for Garden Thyme is a slow grower.

Thyme, Lemon. This is a lovely plant for the house, with its strong, lemony smell. Dig up plants in late September and tear them apart. Re-plant rooted pieces in four-inch square pots, burying all the woody stems. Then clip the tops. A lovely, compact plant will result.

FIELD-GROWN PLANTS

Field-grown Herb plants which you have propagated from material too big to use for pot-grown plants, should be offered for sale directly from the farm, *un*potted. Do not dig them until your customer comes to fetch them. Then:

1. Lift them with a spade, keeping a good ball of soil on the roots.
2. Put them onto a sheet of thin plastic.
3. Gather the plastic up around the stem, tie it with a string, and it's ready to go.

Remember that propagation by layering and division will give you salable plants more quickly than by other methods.

Herbs for Drying

Once your perennial Herbs are well established, you will always have surplus plant material suitable for drying. But to have annual Herbs for drying, you will have to plant them each spring in sufficient quantities to give you a surplus over and above your fresh Herb needs. Remember that it takes three to four pounds of the fresh Herb to make one pound of the dried Herb.

CULINARY HERBS

The markets for dried culinary Herbs are limited for a small grower. The firms that supply the vast food markets with dried Herbs for fragrant teas and for flavor in cooking have large-scale commercial growers to supply their needs.

You will have to concentrate on small-scale, quality production. For example, if you are already supplying chefs with fresh Herbs, you might be able to interest them in buying the dried ones from you, too. You could also specialize in an unusual type of package, selling through gift shops or gourmet food stores, or, if you wanted to keep packaging simple, mail order sales would be a good way to market them. People like to get the dried Herbs they cannot grow themselves directly from a farm.

In the section, "Culinary Products to Make with Dried Herbs," in Chapter 10, you will find all the information you will need and a list of Herbs which should be grown to supply these markets.

COSMETIC HERBS

There are a number of simple cosmetics and toilet waters which can be made with some of the sweet-scented Herbs. Books recommended in Appendix D will be most helpful if you are interested in this area of production.

PERFUME HERBS

The markets for dried perfume Herbs are many, and this is an area of Herb-growing very suitable for the "small" grower, especially one with handicraft skills and a limited growing area.

Do you make ceramics? Why not fill your bowls with potpourri? It can be made from dried or partially dried fragrant flowers and Herbs. Even if you cannot make your own containers, attractive bowls in glass or clear plastic can be found for holding the fragrant mixtures.

Perhaps you are good with a sewing machine or enjoy hand-sewing. An endless variety of Herb pillows and sachets can be made—from the traditional to the bizarre—filled to please the nose or scare the moths away.

TARRAGON, FRENCH (*Artemisia dracunculus*)

Maybe you are not artistic, but can use a sewing machine. Then make plain bags of cheese cloth to package Herbs for hair rinses or for perfuming the bath.

Simple to prepare are dried Herbs to burn as air fresheners. Herb-scented stationery can be made quickly and simply—or it can be a complicated and time-consuming job, depending on the type of finished product you want.

Chapter 10, "Perfumed Products to Make with Dried Herbs," tells what Herbs you need to grow, so that you can make any of the products suggested here. There are also many specialist books on the subject. (See Appendix D.)

A CAT HERB

There is a big market for dried Catnip for cats. It can be sold in packets or loose, but it would be more paying to make Catnip toys. You will find some ideas and suggestions under "Catnip Toys" in Chapter 10.

DYE HERBS

All the Herbs listed at the end of Chapter 9 under "Herbs for Dyes" can be used dried as well as fresh. Also see "Fresh Herbs: Herbs for Dyeing" in this chapter. Talk to your local weavers about their needs. There might be a market for you here.

MEDICINAL HERBS

Many of the Herbs described in this book, both in the basic list in Chapter 3, and in "More Herbs to Grow," (Chapter 9), have medicinal properties. If this aspect of Herb-growing interests you, local natural foods and health food stores should be consulted as to their needs. But, remember that it takes three to four pounds of the fresh to make one pound of the dried.

The large drug houses require their Herbs in vast quantities, and certain concentrations of the active constituents are mandatory. It is unlikely that you would be able to satisfy them until you have gained a great deal of experience, and even then your soil and climate might not be such that it would be possible to obtain these specific constituents in your Herbs.

HERBS FOR LIQUEURS

Like the medicinal Herbs, those used for liqueurs have to be produced in large quantities and to a certain standard. Again, I would say that this is not a market for the beginner or the small-scale grower.

PARSLEY (*Carum petroselinum*)

CHAPTER 7

Growing Parsley

About Different Strains
and Varieties

There are three main types of Parsley: the *curly-leaved*, (essential to chefs for garnish, and used for flavor, too), the *plain-leaved*, (richest in flavor, but uninteresting to look at), and the *turnip-rooted*, (used as a vegetable).

Parsley seed is seldom listed under "Herbs" in seed catalogs, but is usually found in the vegetable section. Most catalogs will have several different kinds of curly Parsley, and new strains are being developed every few years. Try several different kinds for a year or two until you find at least two varieties which suit your needs. We tried fourteen different kinds in our first year! For the fresh Parsley market, you are looking for leaves with a tight curl—and long stems for ease in picking and bunching.

There is another important point to look for, which cannot be ascertained until the plants mature. The first few leaves of all Parsley are without curl, but as the plants grow they produce curly leaves. You will find that some strains of curly Parsley will "throw" a number of plain-leaved plants which *never* develop any curly leaves. Such a variety is wasteful of time and space (if you are growing for chefs), so if you find this trait in a strain you are growing, give it up.

Another type to avoid when you grow for the fresh market is one with "dwarf" in its name. The leaves are beautifully curly, but the stems are short and difficult to pick and bunch. These dwarf strains do make excellent pot plants, however.

111

Varieties of Parsley that stand up to cold well often have "winter" in their names, and it is worth trying a few plants to see how they thrive under your conditions, and if they satisfy your needs. The "winter" types we tried were rather slow-growers, and did not have as tight a curl as the "Moss curled" types.

"French," "Italian," "Plain," and "Perfection" are the plain-leaved varieties; "Hamburg" is the turnip-rooted.

There was no interest in the plain-leaved variety or the turnip-rooted among *our* chefs. However, the plain-leaved type does dry more easily and quickly; it has a very good flavor; and the plants are amazingly prolific. They are usually much more winter-hardy, too, so a few plants are worth growing for yourself.

WHEN WE SOWED FOR THE FRESH HERB MARKET*

When Sowed	Where	When Potted	Planted Out	1st Pick	Last Pick
January 18	Greenhouse	March 1	April 10	May 20	Mid Oct.
February 18	Greenhouse	March 21	April 23	June 1	Mid Oct.

*Note: Our last frost never came after May 24. Our first light frost usually came during the second week of October.

An April sowing will give you a heavy early fall crop, but the dates in the table were the best for *our* market. As the Chive-cutting finished in mid-October, we stopped delivery of Chives *and* Parsley then. These dates coincided with the heaviest demands made by the tourist trade in our local restaurants. Your markets may require different timing, and if so, you will have to adjust your planting and cropping dates.

A July Parsley sowing should produce an early spring crop the next year, though how good it will be depends on the severity of your winter. It is worth trying on a small scale if you have a demand for Parsley in the early spring. Then increase the planting the second year if it has been worthwhile.

There is always a good sale for well-grown Parsley plants in individual pots. The little boxes containing six or eight plants seen in garden shops seldom do well when transplanted into the garden, for after its seedling stage has passed, Parsley does not tolerate any root disturbance.

WHEN WE SOWED FOR POTTED PLANT SALES

When Sowed	Where	Date to Pot	Ready to Sell	Rootbound By
January 18	Greenhouse	March 1	April 10	May 15
February 28	Greenhouse	March 21	April 23	May 30
March 18	Greenhouse	April 20	May 25	June 20

Grow some in the tall 2¼-inch rose pots, and some in 3-inch square pots. Individually grown, these plants can be tapped out of their pots and put into the garden with no root disturbance at all. Be sure to sell them before they are rootbound or they will not grow on well.

Do not plant seed later than mid-March, for by the time the plants are ready to plant out the weather will be too warm for successful transplanting. After potting up the plants, allow a week or so for them to settle down, and when they are showing signs of growing on, harden them off in a cold frame or lath house. Our greenhouse temperatures were too warm for Parsley by mid-April—even in an unheated greenhouse.

You can see by the potted plant table that you will (or should) have plants to sell from April 10 to June 20. (If you want to have Parsley plants for sale at Christmas, plant seed in late August. See also Chapter 6, "Christmas Sales.") These dates may vary a little according to your climate, but they can serve as a guide till you have records of your own.

How to Start Parsley from Seed

Start with fresh seed each year and your germination will be better. I do not recommend direct planting outdoors, since Parsley is a slow and erratic germinator. If you wish to grow first-class curly Parsley, each plant must be given room to grow individually.

Parsley seed should be soaked in warm water for 24 hours before sowing. Follow the directions in Chapter 3, "How to Start Herb Plants from Seed Indoors." Use either the individual pot method or sow in a flat. Personally, I found the individual pots the best, for

when a whole flat of Parsley was ready to transplant, there were too
many seedlings to prick out into pots at one sitting.

As soon as the seedlings are starting to show their first true leaves
they should be potted into tall, 2¼-inch rose pots and grown on in
an unheated greenhouse. Be sure not to delay the final planting out
too long. Tap out a plant now and then, and check on the root
growth. Before the roots have formed a ball, and before the plant is
packed too tightly in the pot, they should be planted out in the beds
eight inches (20 cm.) apart.

Care and Maintenance
of the Parsley Beds

The beds should be prepared as recommended in, "Initial Preparation of the Soil" Chapter 2. Then follow suggestions in "The Final
Preparation of the Soil," up to the point when fertilizer and/or
compost is added. Use *at least* one 40-pound bag of dried steer
manure, or the same amount of well-rotted compost for every 100
square feet of bed, plus two pounds of 6-8-6 fertilizer per 100 square
feet. Use this *as well as* the compost or dried steer manure, not
instead of it.

A regular routine of care and maintenance should be followed to
keep the Parsley growing. A day or two before your first pick, go
over the bed and remove any trash from the outside edges of the
plants. There may be a few yellow leaves—throw them on the
compost heap. There will be outside leaves which are not curly;
these can be bunched and dried (see "Drying Parsley"), but do *not*
be tempted to sell them to your chefs (cheaply) just for flavoring.
Keep your "image" as a quality producer and sell only top-quality,
well-curled leaves.

Next, give the bed a good watering. A day or two after you have
picked the Parsley, clean up the bed and cultivate the soil between
the plants. Remove weeds carefully, for the crowns of Parsley plants
are not very sturdy and will break off with careless handling.

After this cleaning, a liquid fertilizer should be used—*Ra-pid-gro*
or 20-20-20—according to the manufacturers' directions. Organic
gardeners should use a well-diluted liquid manure, but be very
sure that there is no trace of it on the leaves when you ship your next
cut of Parsley. Water well before picking. From three weeks to a

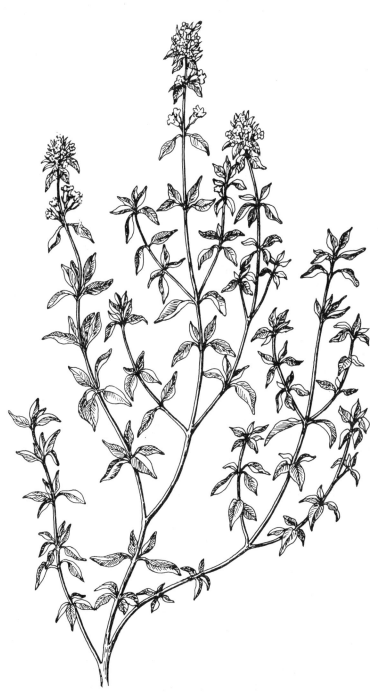

THYME, GARDEN (*Thymus vulgaris*)

115

month later, depending on the time of year, your bed should be ready to pick again.

By late fall, growth will have slowed down or ceased. If your winters are mild, it will be worthwhile to over-winter your Parsley plants. You will get two or three cuts from them in spring before they go to seed (remember, Parsley is a biennial). In climates with a cold winter, the plants should be treated as annuals, dug out in the fall and the beds cleaned up to lie fallow over the winter. The same beds should not be used more often than once every three years for Parsley.

Harvesting the Parsley

We sowed according to the dates under "Parsley for the Fresh Herb Market," and it was ready for a first pick from about the middle to the end of May. "Picking" is really a misnomer, since it is necessary to catch hold of the stalk, lean it back, and pull with one hand, while holding the thick central stem with the other hand to prevent it breaking. The stalk will then come off at the junction with the central stem, and will leave no piece behind to rot. It takes a little practice to get it right, but is worth the effort. The next picking will be made easier if you pick it this way.

Put 10 to 15 stems in a bunch and slip on a rubber band. When you have about 10 bunches, take them to a cool place and stand them in a plastic bowl (never use metal ones; they will discolor the Parsley), with water covering the stems, but not the leaves.

Go back and pick another ten bunches and put them in water. Repeat this until you have picked enough for your orders. The Parsley should be left standing in water for several hours—preferably overnight; this will give you crisp leaves and a fresh appearance, which the Parsley will retain for days.

Package the Parsley in plastic bags holding five pounds or less—never more—or it will crush. Get it to your customers as quickly as you can after taking it out of the water. Sell it by weight, but be very careful to shake well before packing, since nobody wants to pay for water!

Note: To keep Parsley crisp and fresh for your own use in the house, stand its stems in cold water (like cut flowers). Do not refrigerate it.

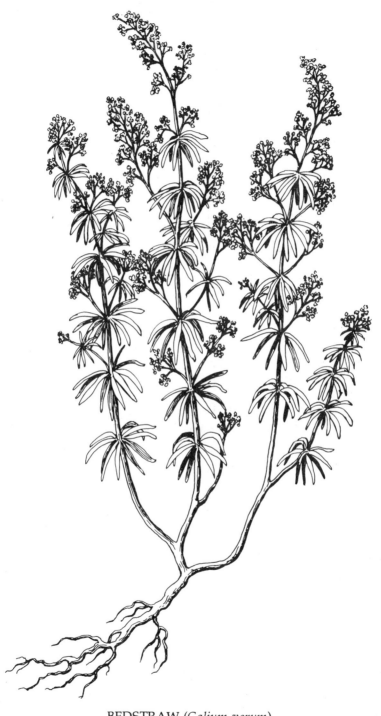

BEDSTRAW (*Galium verum*)

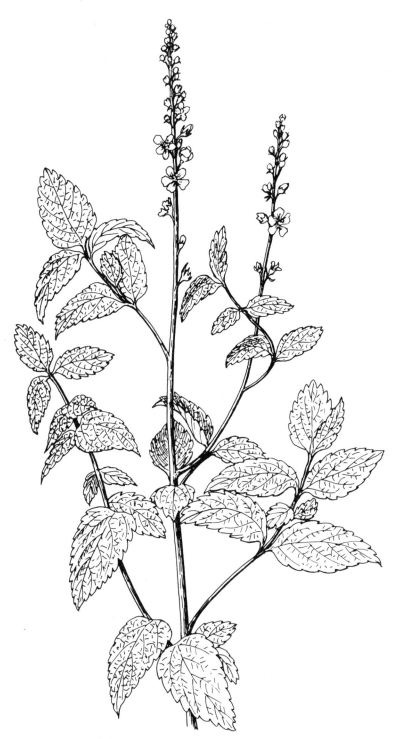

AGRIMONY (*Agrimonia eupatoria*)

Drying the Parsley

Curly Parsley is one of the few Herbs which *must* have a little artificial heat to dry it. For small quantities an oven at 100° F. (38° C.) will do a quick and efficient job. Larger quantities can be dried as described in Chapter 5, "How to Dry Herbs," but temperatures should be a little higher than for all other Herbs.

The plain-leaved Parsley will dry in warm, dry weather without artificial heat, provided the humidity is low.

Pricing Fresh Parsley

Local produce wholesalers may be willing to quote you current prices for Parsley sold to local stores, but it will probably be by the dozen bunches and not by weight. Ask the manager of your local produce store if he will weigh 12 bunches for you, so that you can work out prices by weight. Explain to him what you are doing; he is a good man to get to know.

The price which you ask your chefs to pay should be at least as much as this retail price in the stores. So you will be selling in wholesale quantities and getting a retail price. This is your bonus for good-quality curl.

Remembering that your chefs will be paying top prices, take them only a top-quality product. To do this you will almost certainly have to put aside quite a lot of otherwise good Parsley. If you do not want to dry it, find a produce store that will buy it. Even without the curl it is still good for flavoring. You will, of course, only get the much lower wholesale price for it. *Don't* sell it to your chefs at a lower price "just for flavor."

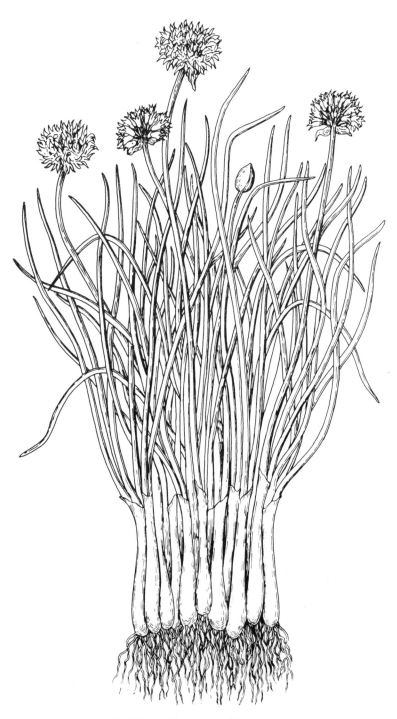

CHIVES (*Allium schoenoprasum*)

CHAPTER 8

Growing Chives

I am assuming that you intend starting your Chives from seed. It is most unlikely that you will be able to find—let alone afford—enough Chive plants to start you growing them on a big enough scale to supply any restaurants.

I cannot give you an accurate estimate of the number of plants *you* will need to yield a certain number of pounds of "greens" all season long. Much depends on your skill, your soil, your facilities for watering, and the weather. But to give you some guidance, I will detail exactly what *we* did, and *our* results. Remember that we were on the southern tip of Vancouver Island, in British Columbia, where spring comes early (for Canada), falls are long and often mild, and only occasional winters are cold (and even these are mild compared with other parts of Canada). Our rainfall was heavy, but usually July and August were dry—sometimes very dry.

We usually started cutting in late March, sometimes early April, and continued through spring and summer into fall; the last cut usually was made in mid-October—a six-and-a-half to seven-month season.

If I sound a little dogmatic and opinionated in this chapter (or other chapters on growing instructions) I apologize. I am trying to pass on to you explicit instructions which I *know* work. You may find that others are better for you, but until you gain experience, try our ways—they are proven. You will save yourself a lot of headaches, and probably money, too.

Preparation of the Beds

Prepare the Chive beds according to suggestions in Chapter 2 ("Final Preparation of the Soil"), *adding at least one and a half bags* (60 pounds) of dried steer manure per 100 square feet of bed (or the same amount of compost) before the final run over with the rototiller or before the final raking. This may sound a lot to use, but remember that the plants will be in those beds for three years, and it is much easier to work the soil before any planting is done. It will still be necessary to add more humus to the soil as time goes on, but a thorough preparation at this early stage will benefit the plants all their lives. You cannot put in too much organic matter. The addition of an onion fertilizer is recommended at this stage too. Follow the advice of your local Agricultural Extension Agent on quantities.

Starting from Seed

Seed may be sown any time between April and September–March if you have a greenhouse. A spring planting is most practical.

Standard indoor procedure for sowing should be followed, (Chapter 3, "How to Start Herb Plants from Seed Indoors,") but the seed is sown very thickly in the flats. Optimum temperature for germination is 60° to 80° F. (15° to 26° C.).

When the little plants are a few inches high, and the roots have spread and become a little bit matted, the whole contents of the flat, Chives, soil and roots, can be cut into two-inch squares and planted

Cutting a flat of Chives into two-inch (5 cm.) squares.

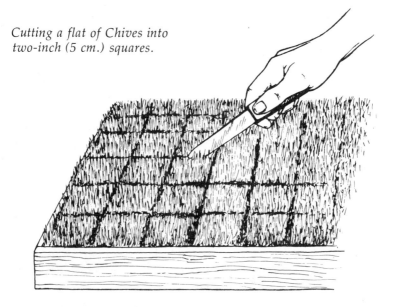

out, the same depth as they were in the seed box. Allow eight inches (20 cm.) from center to center of plants.

Little work needs to be done beyond regular watering and weeding. But get down on your hands and knees and lift the perennial weeds (especially grasses) right out by their roots. This will save much time and frustration when you start to harvest the next year.

You are not likely to get a large cut the first year, even after a spring sowing. So don't make any commitments till you see what you have. Late in the fall the greens will die down, and the plants will not show all winter long. Don't worry. With the first sign of spring (or even before) they will start to come through again. By late March or early April you will be taking your first big harvest.

Care and Maintenance of the Beds

Follow this routine after every cut:

1. Weed the bed thoroughly and cultivate with a hand cultivator around the plants. At the same time, trim the grass edge, if you have grass paths.
2. Put at least one 40-pound bag of dried steer manure per 100 square feet around the plants, but do not cover the plants themselves. Do not rake it in, rather leave it on the surface to form a mulch, and it will gradually disappear into the soil.
3. Water the beds well, adding a little liquid manure, *Ra-pid-gro,* or 20-20-20 to the water. Follow the maker's recommendation as to strength of the last two. This must be done immediately after cutting and before there is any sign of new growth starting.
4. Two days before the next cut, water the beds well. They must have time to dry before the cutting is done.

In the fall, when growth has stopped and plants have died down, apply compost at the rate of about 40 pounds per 100 square feet of bed—more if you have it.

In the spring, as soon as the new growth begins to show, apply 6-8-6 fertilizer at the rate of two pounds per 100 square feet.

BASIL, BUSH (*Ocimum minimum*)

124

Replanting Older Beds

You should be able to cut from your beds for at least three seasons after planting them out, before they need to be replanted. So four years after putting in seedlings, or three years after dividing plants, you will have to consider digging out and replanting the bed. You will find then that when you dig up a plant the roots have spread, and probably are getting entangled with the next-door plants.

Your best tool for lifting the plants is a small, well-sharpened spade, such as a "lady's planting spade." It is worthwhile getting this sharpened professionally.

Your plants should be dug a few at a time, roots trimmed and as much soil as possible removed. The plants are then split into three or four parts, most of the greens cut off, and the roots trimmed again to half-an-inch in length; hold them in a tight bunch, and make a small hole in the soil. Plant them eight inches apart, pressing the soil gently around them, so that only about half an inch shows above the surface of the soil.

With two of you working on this operation, it is amazing how fast the new beds get planted. One should dig and do the initial trimming, and the other split the plants and replant. Unless the weather is damp, it is a good idea to water (preferably overhead irrigation) within the next few days. "Puddling in" on this scale is impractical.

This replanting can be done as soon as the plants begin to show in the early spring, on through April, May and June. If the months of July and August are dry, don't do it then. But early September is good, since there is then time for the plants to get well rooted before the winter starts. There is a theory that late fall planting is quite all right, but we found that should you have an early frost before the plants have had time to put out new roots and secure themselves, the frost will heave them up, and you will have a long and laborious job pressing them in again. In practice, we found a mid-May replanting the best, and we were cutting for sale within five weeks!

This is the time to pot up a few dozen plants. See "A Bonus from Your Chive Beds," at the end of this chapter.

Harvesting

Get these things ready before you start:

1. Something waterproof to kneel on—standing and bending double for hours at a time is very tiring, and a strain on your back—so kneel.
2. A Stanley knife with replaceable blades—stainless steel if obtainable. Change the blade as soon as it begins to "tug," rather than slice, through the Chives. A blunt knife damages the plants and slows up the work.
3. Number 10 rubber bands to put around each little bunch of Chives, as you cut them. Be sure the bands have no objectionable rubbery smell.
4. Plastic bags to put the harvested Chives in. Either the five- or seven-pound size, with a side pleastt or gusset, holds one pountd of the cut and cleaned Herb. The seven-pound size is needed only if and when you have a very tall crop to cut.
5. Scales for weighing. Sell by weight, not by the bunch, since bunches are impossible to make up to an exact thickness or length, and the plants vary in size according to their age and the time of year.
6. Styrofoam coolers to keep the cut Chives cool.
7. Enough frozen "jelly" bags (as used in picnic coolers) to keep the coolers' temperatures down.
8. A table and chairs (inside when it's cold, in the shade of a tree in warmer weather) to sit at as you do the cleaning and packaging.

HOW TO CUT THE CHIVES

It is most important to cut the Chives when they are dry, for wet Chives go slimy quickly, even under refrigeration.

1. Put your left hand (reverse instructions for a left-handed person) half way up the bunch of growing Chive greens. With the Stanley knife in your right hand, slice through the greens about half-an-inch from ground level. Never cut the tips off Chives, always cut at ground level, even if you need only a few

CHAMOMILE, ENGLISH or ROMAN (*Anthemis nobilis*)

for your own use. This stimulates the growth. Cutting the tips of *growing* Chives does not.
2. Slip a rubber band around them.
3. Put them in the cooler.
4. At this stage don't worry about bits of grass and weeds amongst the Chives. When the cooler is full, take it to the table—you will be glad to get off your knees by now!

HOW TO CLEAN THE CHIVES

From the first cut, and possibly the second, you will have little or no trash, and little or no cleaning will be necessary. But when it is:

1. Take off the rubber band, and, holding the Chives close to the tips, shake gently, and the grass and weeds will fall out. It may be necessary to trim a little of the base stems off the bottom of the Chives to free the trash.
2. Slip the rubber band back on the clean Chives.

Note: At some periods of the growing season there will be a lot of trash to clean out. There may be yellowing tips to trim off, flower heads and stems (which are very tough) to be pulled out, weeds and grass which have grown up in the older clumps, however careful you have been with the weeding, and even a few Chive greens which don't look perfect. *Remove all this.* The chefs and salad-makers only want to chop up the Chives—not clean them. Send out good quality, clean Chives, and you will get a good price for them—and repeat orders.

HOW TO PACKAGE THE CHIVES

As soon as the rubber band is on the clean Chives:

1. Package the Chives in the five- or seven-pound bags, one pound to a bag. Close with "Twistems" and put in a cooler.
2. Transfer to an ordinary household refrigerator as soon as possible. *Never freeze Chives.*

Pricing

Pricing is one of the most difficult things to get right. We were fortunate in knowing a very cooperative chef, and by various calculations with amounts and prices of green onions, we fixed on $3.50 per pound in 1966. Early in 1974 we were getting $5 per pound, and the price was due for another rise the next year—but by then we had retired. So, calculate your prices on a comparative basis.

You will find that the ordinary, everyday family restaurant is not likely to pay these prices—in fact, many of them don't even think there is any point in having Chives, as their clients "wouldn't know the difference between Chives and green onions!" You will have to go to the more exclusive restaurants, whose chefs and customers do "know their onions!"

When you go to see a chef for the first time, take along a packet of Chives (say half a pound), and tell him you would like him to try them, and see how far they will go—before giving an order. Every chef we did this for was amazed how far they *did* go.

Go to the kitchen entrance and ask what time it would be convenient for you to speak to the chef. Go back later, if necessary, but *don't* give or show your sample to anyone else if you can possibly help it. The chef will be the man who makes the decision whether to continue using green onions or to switch to your Chives. If he isn't the man who makes the decisions in the kitchen, then you are probably at the wrong restaurant! We found that whenever the owner or manager made these decisions, it was usually "no." The chefs who really rule their kitchens are the men you want.

Having got hold of the right man, tell him the price per pound, the day *you* prefer to deliver (does it suit him?), and that you sell them in pound packets. To begin with, we did make up half pound packets, but as our market grew we found it uneconomical to do so. But don't pack them in lots bigger than one pound, or they won't keep so well. Having only one size of bag also makes the deliveries less complicated.

Delivering

It may not be possible to cut all you need for your weekly orders in one day. In this case, what you do cut may be held over in an ordinary household refrigerator till all are cut and ready to deliver. Keep them cool from the beginning of harvest to the moment you hand them in to your chef. Pack them in a styrofoam cooler for their trip to the restaurant, not forgetting to put in the frozen "jelly bags." You can tell your chefs with perfect confidence that they will keep for two to three weeks in his refrigerator. During the third week, the flavor may deteriorate a little, but there is no need to stress this point! He shouldn't need to keep them so long anyway. He should be able to calculate how much he needs each week, though he may want to carry extra for emergencies. But with a high-priced item like Chives, it is well that he knows they *will* keep if he over-orders. If he knows this, he is unlikely to ask you to deliver more than once a week. You are unlikely to have the time in the busy spring and summer months, so don't agree to do so.

Again remember that if cut wet, Chives are impossible to clean properly, and they will not keep for more than a few days.

Your chefs and salad-makers will continue to be your happy customers if your Chives are clean and ready to chop up. Never sell them ready-chopped; you won't be paid any more for them, and it takes a lot of time to chop large quantities. When chopped Chives are stored for more than a few hours, there is a loss of flavor, too.

Yields

As noted at the beginning of this chapter, I cannot tell you what yields *you* will get, but I can give you some idea of what you can expect, based on figures we obtained after several years' experience.

Two thousand plants, some three years old, others two, gave approximately 30 to 40 pounds of fresh Chives each week, from first cut in spring through early summer, by cutting from 500 to 700 plants each week. To put it another way, each plant was cut once every three or four weeks.

Through July and August, which for us were usually hot, dry months, the plants yielded less (in spite of good irrigation), for Chives grow better in the cooler months. This was the time when the new, May-planted beds came into production, which enabled us to keep up with our heavy summer orders. From mid-September on, the cuts became lighter, till growth ceased altogether by late fall.

When we asked various chefs how far the Chives went in the kitchens, they said that they were far more economical than green onions (and far superior, of course). Depending on how generous (or how mean) they were, they could "stretch" a pound of chopped Chives to serve 300 to 400 baked potatoes, but they couldn't estimate quantities for salads and other dishes.

Small specialty restaurants probably will take only a pound of Chives a week, but if you are supplying chefs in large hotels—especially those that cater to banquets and gourmet dining clubs—they may order 10 pounds or more a week. (The same proportions apply to Parsley, the small restaurants using two or three pounds a week, the larger ones 20 to 30 pounds or more.)

A Bonus from Your Chive Beds

WHEN YOU HAVE CHIVE PLANTS
TO SPARE

There will come a time, though it is hard to believe in the first years, when you will have Chive plants to spare.

When you are digging three- or four-year-old plants to divide, put aside some for potting up for sale as Chive plants. Twenty of these older plants are enough to make up at least 100 potted plants. But remember that as long as you have chefs still asking for more Chives, *large-scale* sales of Chive plants are not as profitable as increasing your beds for cutting.

So sell a limited number of Chive plants to your regular retail outlets, and if you sell at your place at retail, have a few for *normal* small retail sales. There is the risk that somebody who wants to buy several hundred plants may be planning to go into the fresh Chive business—and unless you are close to a very big market, there probably won't be room for two of you.

PREPARING CHIVES FOR SALE AS PLANTS

1. Dig plants as suggested under "Replanting beds." Shake off the soil, trim the roots, and divide into groups of eight to 10 bulblets. Trim off most of the greens, and again shorten the roots, this time to about a half inch in length.

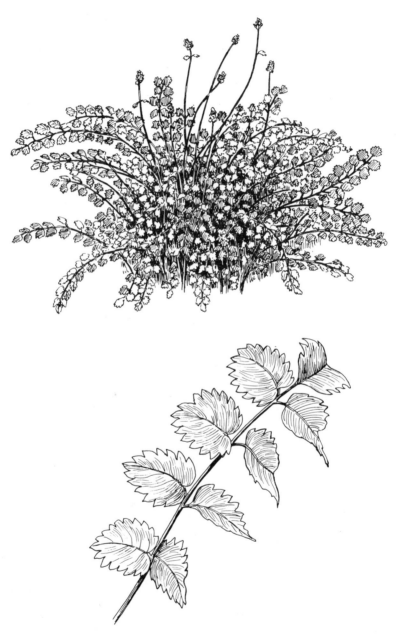

BURNET, SALAD (*Poterium sanguisorba*)

2. Loosely fill four-inch square plastic pots with potting soil.
3. Make a hole in the middle, and press the little bunch of Chives in, shaking the pot to settle the soil.
4. Water, preferably with *Ra-pid-gro* or 20-20-20, following the makers' instructions.
5. Leave in lath house or greenhouse, according to weather and time of year.
6. Keep moist, but do not over-water, especially in winter.

The dates below will give you an indication of when to plant, to get Chive plants for sale when demands are highest.

Date We Divided and Potted	Where Held	Date When Our Plants Were Ready to Sell
February 14	Greenhouse	In 3 weeks—March 7
March 1	Greenhouse	In 3 weeks—March 21
March 1	Greenhouse/lath house	In 5 weeks—April 5
March 15	Lath house	In 6 weeks—April 30
November 10	Greenhouse	In 4 weeks—Dec. 8-22

Note: If some of the plants potted up on March 1st are transferred to the lath house after ten days, a batch will be ready to sell about April 5th. Move them in the morning, choosing, if possible, a dry sunny day to lessen the shock of temperature change.

From these dates, you can see how the warmth in the greenhouse speeds up the growth. However, from April onwards our greenhouse was too warm for Chives.

The first two lots which had heat in the greenhouse were well—though not fully—grown, and were quite suitable for early sales. The third and fourth lots were fully grown plants with four to six inches of growth on them. The first two lots supplied people who were too impatient to wait for the sturdier and cool-grown plants!

CALENDULA or POT MARIGOLD (*Calendula officinalis*)

CHAPTER 9

Thirty-two More Herbs
to Grow

A Few Suggestions

When your basic Herb garden is growing well, and you are able to propagate from it, you can start growing a greater variety of Herbs.

In this chapter, 32 other Herbs are listed alphabetically (under their common names), and all the horticultural data you need to grow them is given. This data includes the Latin name, whether the Herb is perennial, biennial, or annual, and if it is hardy or tender to frost. The height of the mature plant is also given, and the type of soil and situation in which it thrives best. Often the Herbs will adapt to other types of soil and situations, so give them a chance, even if you can't create ideal conditions. Methods of propagation will be indicated, and planting distances, too. Some of the uses to which the Herbs are put are given also.

You may not want to grow many of these Herbs on a large scale, but you will want to have stock plants from which to propagate plants for sale. I would suggest that now is the time to start your formal Herb garden, both for your own education and for the benefit of visiting customers.

If you are thinking of selling plants retail at your place, a formal Herb garden will be an invaluable sales aid. It is of great interest to customers to see what their own plants will look like in a year or two. People are much more inclined to buy unfamiliar Herbs if they can see how they will look when mature. They may see just the thing for an odd corner in their garden which needs filling, but the same immature plant in its pot in the lath house would not have inspired them to buy. Remember, however, that once you open this garden to your customers, you will have to be on hand to show it to them, and this can take up a lot of time.

We laid out a formal garden, with wide paths between semicircular beds, and each plant was clearly labelled with its Latin and common name. No need, we thought, to take customers around; we could get on with our work while they wandered alone. However, it didn't turn out this way—they all expected a conducted tour, and wanted endless questions answered!

INDEX OF 32 MORE HERBS TO GROW

We kept this garden open to the public for several years, but each year visitors took up more and more time. Finally, deciding to give up all retail sales from the farm, we also closed the garden.

If you decide on a formal Herb garden I suggest you plant it with all the Herbs in the basic list in Chapter 3, and as many of the Herbs as you can obtain from the list which follows in this chapter. It will take 18 months to two years before it will be ready to show to customers and by that time you should know enough about all of these Herbs to be able to answer most of the questions you will be asked.

However, if you decide that you cannot spare the time for visitors, do not feel that the time and energy you have put into creating the garden has been wasted. You will have learned much about the Herbs, you will have a garden from which you can obtain material to propagate, and finally, caring for a garden like this can be a great pleasure and a change from routine work.

If, on the other hand, you decide to open the garden to visitors, remember that it must never be neglected, however busy you are. It is your "shop window."

How To Grow
the 32 More Herbs

Agrimony (*Agrimonia eupatoria*) a hardy perennial which grows from 24 to 36 inches (60 to 90 cm.) in height.

It prefers well-drained, ordinary soil, and some shade.

Propagation is by seed, though germination is difficult, or by root cuttings in spring or fall.

Plants should stand 10 inches (25 cm.) apart.

It is used in medicine, in dyeing, and in making a refreshing tea.

Alkanet (*Alkanna tinctoria*) a hardy perennial growing to a height of almost 24 inches (60 cm.).

It prefers a light, sandy, well-drained soil, and some sun.

Propagation is by seed (established plants self-sow), also by root cuttings in spring.

Plants should stand about 18 inches (45 cm.) apart.

It is used as a dye plant.

Basil, Bush (*Ocimum minimum*) is a half-hardy annual, growing 8 inches (20 cm.) high.

It prefers a well-drained, rich soil, and full sun.

Propagation is by seed, in the spring, at a temperature of *at least* 60° F. (15° C.).

Plants should stand 12 inches (30 cm.) apart.

It is used for flavor, like Sweet Basil, but makes a more attractive and compact pot plant. Basils all act as fly repellents.

Bay (*Laurus nobilis*), sometimes known as Bay Laurel or Sweet Bay.

It is a perennial, and, although tender for the first few years of its life, will stand a few degrees of frost when mature. It can reach a height of 20 feet (6 meters) when fully grown.

In many areas it is better to grow it in tubs in a sunny, sheltered position; in winter it should be given protection, either in the greenhouse or a frost-free shed or cool basement under 45° F. (about 7° C.), watering only enough to prevent it from completely drying out.

Bay needs plenty of sun and good drainage, but is not particular as to soil. John Innes number 2 mixture is suitable for pot growing Bay.

Propagation is by seed sown in spring—also by cuttings taken in late summer and kept moist (by mist if possible), and given bottom heat. Layering may be done in late summer also.

If Bay thrives in your climate, it is unlikely you will need more than one tree. If grown in pots, start them in five-inch sizes, and re-pot in the spring to larger ones if they are becoming root-bound. Once large enough to need tubs, they should not be repotted except to renew exhausted soil.

Bay is used for flavor and in medicine.

Bedstraw (*Galium verum*) a hardy perennial plant growing three feet (90 cm.) high.

It prefers a dry, sandy soil, and full sun.

Propagation is by seed in fall, by running roots lifted and replanted in spring.

Plants should stand 24 inches (60 cm.) apart.

It is used as a dye plant, for wool and butter(!), and also to curdle milk. It has medicinal uses.

BAY (*Laurus nobilis*)

BERGAMOT (*Monarda didyma* and *fistulosa*)

Bergamots (*Monarda didyma* and *fistulosa*) are hardy perennial plants, both growing to a height of 36 inches (90 cm.) or more.

They prefer a moist, ordinary soil, in sun or some shade.

Propagation is by seed, and by division of plants, which should always be done in the spring.

Plants should stand 18 inches (45 cm.) apart.

They are used to make teas, in the cosmetic and perfume industries, and they also have medicinal properties.

Burnet, Salad (*Poterium sanguisorba*). There is some confusion over the naming of this plant, but this *is* the *salad* Burnet.

A hardy perennial growing about 18 inches (45 cm.) high, it prefers a dry, ordinary soil, and full sun.

Propagation is by seed in fall, as soon as they are ripe. It self-sows freely, and the seedlings can be moved when small.

Plants should be 12 inches (30 cm.) apart.

It is used as an ingredient in salads, when the leaves are young and tender, to give a cucumber flavor.

Calendula or Pot Marigold (*Calendula officinalis*) is a hardy annual growing to a height of 24 inches (60 cm.).

It prefers a well-drained, light, sandy soil, in full sun.

It is propagated by seed in fall or spring.

Plants should stand 12 inches (30 cm.) apart.

The flower heads are used in soups and stews, and the yellow dye extracted to give butter a good color. It also has medicinal properties.

Chamomile, English or Roman (*Anthemis nobilis*) is a low-growing hardy perennial. Its flower stems will reach a height of 12 inches (30 cm.), but if it is kept clipped to ground level it will form an excellent ground cover. It prefers a well-drained, light soil, and full sun.

It can be propagated by seed, which is slow to germinate, or by division of the plants. Tiny rooted pieces can also be cut off established plants and replanted.

Plants should be planted in a clean, weed-free area, 6 inches (15 cm.) apart.

The flower heads are used in medicine, and in the cosmetic and perfume industries.

Chamomile, German (*Matricaria chamomilla*) is a hardy annual, growing to a height of 24 inches (60 cm.) or more. It prefers a well-drained, sandy soil, and full sun.

Propagation is by seed, which germinates easily, and it self-sows freely. Thin plants to about eight inches (20 cm.) apart.

The flower heads are used to make Chamomile tea, which has medicinal properties.

Do not confuse this Chamomile with the English or Roman variety, above. Both have medicinal properties, but only the English or Roman is suitable for a ground cover.

Elecampane (*Inula helenium*) is a hardy perennial, growing to a height of 96 inches (2.40 m.) or more.

It prefers a moist, lightish soil, and full sun.

It is propagated by seed, or by pieces of root, severed so that each piece has a bud on it, and planted 30 inches apart in a warm, sandy soil, in early summer.

It is used in medicine and in the production of some liqueurs.

Horehound (*Marubium vulgaris*) is a hardy perennial (though in-clined to winter kill if in a damp location) growing to a height of 24 inches (60 cm.) or more.

It prefers a dry, light and sandy soil, and full sun, though it will tolerate some shade.

Propagation is by seed, sown in spring; it may take as long as three weeks to germinate. Also by root division in spring.

Plants should stand ten inches (25 cm.) apart.

It is used in medicine, especially in cough candy. It can also be used to supply the bitter ingredient when making homemade beer.

Hyssop (*Hyssopus officinalis*) is a hardy perennial, growing about 18 inches (45 cm.) high.

It prefers well-drained, well limed, lightish soil and full sun, though will tolerate partial shade.

Propagation is by seed, division of plants in spring, or by cuttings.

Plants should stand 12 inches (30 cm.) apart.

It is used in medicine and in the manufacture of some liqueurs and perfumes; it is said to repel insects.

ELECAMPANE (*Inula helenium*)

(A) SPEARMINT (*Mentha spicata var. Viridis*)
(B) VARIEGATED APPLE MINT (*Mentha rotundifolia variegata*)
(C) BERGAMOT or ORANGE MINT (*Mentha citrata*)

Lovage (*Levisticum officinale*) is a hardy perennial, which sometimes grows as high as 84 inches (2 m.).

It prefers a moist, well-enriched soil, and some shade.

Propagation is by seed, as soon as it is ripe in fall, and by division of the clumps as the shoots start to show in spring.

Plants should stand at least 36 inches (90 cm.) apart.

It is used for flavoring in the kitchen; its taste resembles a very pungent celery. It has medicinal uses, and is also used in the perfume trade. The dried leaves are used to make a fragrant tea—but it is not to everybody's taste!

Madder (*Rubia tinctorum*) is a hardy perennial. Though the stems grow as long as 48 inches (1.20 m.), they are decumbent, and lie close to the ground.

It prefers a light, sandy, well-drained soil, and full sun.

Propagation is by seed, by division of roots, and by runners.

Plants should be placed about ten inches (25 cm.) apart, but soon meet, since they spread by underground runners.

The roots are used for dyeing. It also has medicinal properties.

Three Mints (*Mentha* various). There are many varieties of Mints, but these three (with the two in the basic list) are all good sellers. Spearmint (*Mentha spicata*, var. *Viridis*), Variegated Apple Mint (*Mentha rotundifolia varigata*), and Bergamot, or Orange, Mint (*Mentha citrata*). All are hardy perennials, growing about 36 inches (90 cm.) high.

They prefer rich, moist soil. Shade is only essential if the location is somewhat dry. Avoid manure, since it causes a disease called rust, which cannot be cured, and affected plants have to be destroyed.

Propagation is quick and easy—by runners, planted out in spring or fall, six inches (15 cm.) apart and two inches (5 cm.) deep.

The Variegated Apple Mint has delicate green leaves with creamy variegations and is purely ornamental.

Spearmint is used medicinally, in the kitchen, in toothpastes, chewing gum, and many products which need a minty flavor. The smell of Bergamot Mint is reputed to keep mice away, and it is used in medicine and in the perfume industry.

Don't just buy a "Mint." Many have a tendency to revert to a rank odor and taste. Be sure to buy named varieties.

Mullein (*Verbascum thapsus*) is a hardy biennial growing as much as 96 inches (2.4 m.) high in cultivation, in its second year.
    Thrives in poor, dry soil, in any location.
    Propagation is by seed, and it self-sows very freely.
    Small seedlings may be transplanted, leaving a space of 18 inches (45 cm.) to 24 inches (60 cm.) between them.
    It is used in medicine, and is a good dye plant.

Pennyroyal (*Mentha pulegium*). This is the ENGLISH Pennyroyal, which is a hardy perennial with a prostrate creeping habit. There is an upright type also, but seed is hard to get.
    It prefers a moist, heavy soil, in partial shade.
    Propagation is by seed in spring, or by removal and resetting of the tiny, rooted stems in spring or fall, about 6 inches (15 cm.) apart.
    It is used in medicine and as a tea, and is reputed to repel fleas.
    It also makes a very good ground cover, in moist, heavy soils.
    American Pennyroyal (*Hedeoma pulegioides*) is a hardy annual which has similar uses, but is not suitable for ground cover, since it grows some 10 inches (25 cm.) high.

Pyrethrum (*Chrysanthemum cinerariaefolium*). This is the "Insect Powder Plant," and is a hardy perennial, growing to a height of 18-24 inches (45-60 cm.).
    It prefers a well-drained, well-limed soil, in full sun.
    The single white flower heads are more desirable than other colors or types.
    Propagation is by seed, also by division of two year or older plants.
    Plants should stand 18 inches (45 cm.) apart.
    Pyrethrum, used in many insecticides, is harmless to humans and animals.
    For more information about Pyrethrum write to: Pyrethrum Information Center, Room 423, 744 Broad Street, Newark, New Jersey 07012.

Rose Geranium (*Pelargonium graveolens*) is a half-hardy perennial, which needs a greenhouse, unless you are in an area quite free from frost.
    It prefers a well-drained, lightish soil, with plenty of sun.

MULLEIN (*Verbascum thapsus*)

147

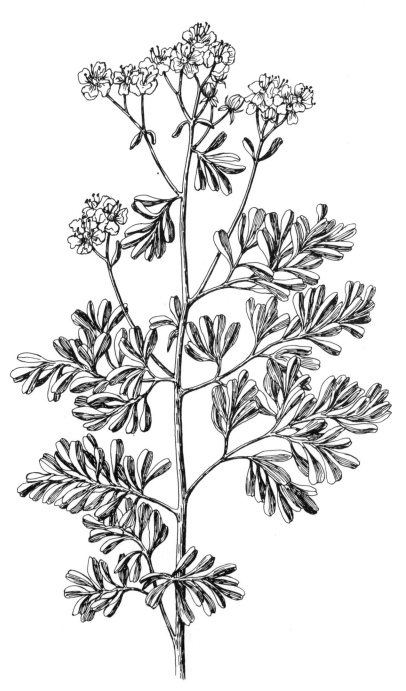

RUE (*Ruta graveolens*)

It can be propagated from seed, and is also propagated from cuttings.

If planted in the garden, mature plants will need to be 36 inches (90 cm.) apart.

It is used in the perfume industry. It can be used as a flavoring for cakes; put the leaves on the bottom of the tin, pour the cake batter over them, and bake as usual.

Rue *(Ruta graveolens)* a hardy perennial, growing 24 inches (60 cm.) high. It needs a well-drained, poor soil. It is liable to winter kill in a heavy, damp soil.

Propagation is by seed, sown in spring, and by cuttings taken in spring.

The plants should stand about 24 inches (60 cm.) apart.

It is used in medicine, the cosmetic industry, and the smell of it is a deterrent to flies.

Saffron Crocus *(Crocus sativus)*. This tiny, 3-inch (7 cm.) high plant grows from a corm.

The soil should be well drained, well worked, and rich, and the situation may be in full sun or part shade.

Propagation is by the little corms, which should be planted 6 inches (15 cm.) apart. It can be started from seed, which is difficult to obtain, and it will take three years or more to produce the corms, which; in their turn, will produce the flowers.

To produce one gram of Saffron, requires the stigmas and styles of about 150 flowers! It is used for color and flavor in the kitchen, in medicine, and if you can grow enough—it is a wonderful yellow dye for wool and silk.

Santolina or Lavender Cotton *(Santolina chamaecyparissus)*. A hardy perennial growing 24 inches (60 cm.) high.

It prefers a well-drained, light, dry soil, and full sun.

Propagation by seed is possible, but slow, while cuttings root easily, and branches may be layered in summer.

Plants should stand 36 inches (90 cm.) apart.

It is used in medicine, as an insecticide (especially against moths) and in the perfume industry.

Sorrel, French *(Rumex scutatus)*. A hardy perennial, which can be distinguished from other Sorrels by its leaves, which are almost heart-shaped, succulent, fleshy and somewhat brittle. Its taste is acid, but not unpleasantly so.

It prefers a moist, rich, and heavy soil, and full sun.

Propagation is by seed: treat as a hardy annual.

The plants should stand about 18 inches (45 cm.) apart.

Be sure to get the right variety. There are many types of *Rumex*, and *R. scutatus* is the only one which is not too acid to go into salads and soups.

Southernwood or Old Man *(Artemisia abrotanum)*. A hardy perennial growing about 36 inches (90 cm.) high. It thrives in almost any soil, and full sun.

It is propagated by cuttings, which root easily.

The mature plants should stand 48 inches (1.20 m.) apart.

It is used as a moth deterrent, and has some medicinal properties. It is very ornamental if kept pruned.

Tansy *(Tanacetum vulgare)*. A hardy perennial growing some 36 inches (90 cm.) high. It thrives in any soil, but requires a well-drained situation, with plenty of sun.

It can be propagated by seed, or by division in spring or fall.

It should be planted 48 inches (1.20 m.) apart, where it will not encroach on other plants, as it is a quick spreader.

It is used in medicine, in the cosmetic and liqueur industries, and as a preservative. It is a good dye plant, and insect repellent.

Thymes, Various *(Thymus* species). There are many varieties of Thyme, apart from the two already mentioned in the basic lists. All are perennial, and many hardy.

They vary in height, from the prostrate and creeping varieties, such as the *serpyllums* and *doerfleri,* through the semi-prostrate *T. herba-barona* with its long, arching stems, *T. erectus* like a miniature yew tree a few inches high, to the bush types, varying in height from 6 inches (15 cm.) to 12 inches (30 cm.) high.

All Thymes require a light, sandy, well-limed and well-drained soil, and need full sun.

They can *all* be propagated by cuttings during spring and summer. In spring or fall, creeping varieties (including all varieties of *T. serpyllum*) can also be divided. Bushy Thymes can be stool layered.

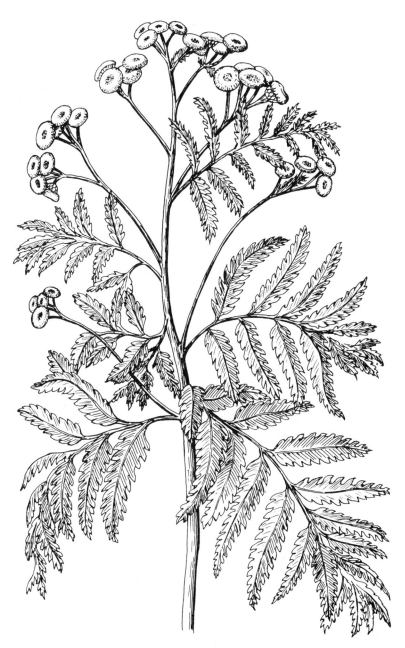

TANSY (*Tanacetum vulgare*)

VERBENA, LEMON (*Lippia citriodora*)

The planting distance varies according to the type—the bush needing about 12 inches (30 cm.), the upright about 8 inches (20 cm.), and the creeping types 4 inches (10 cm.).

Few of these Thymes have culinary use, except the *T. herba-barona*, which can be used to flavor roast beef. All are very ornamental, and some delightfully perfumed. The low-growing *T. serpyllums* quickly form a close mat and cover the ground. When planted in the cracks of a stone or brick path they grow quickly, and the effect is unusual and pleasing.

Verbena, Lemon *(Lippia citriodora)* is a not-quite-hardy perennial. Though the mature plant will stand some frost, especially in climates with low humidity, it is best to treat it as a half-hardy perennial, and give it some winter protection. Either winter it in a greenhouse, or cut it back in late fall and winter it in a cool basement, watering it infrequently. In a frost-free climate it will grow to a height of 72 to 96 inches (1.80 to 2.40 m.).

It prefers a light, well-drained soil, and full sun.

It is propagated by cuttings, taken when shoots of about 4 inches (10 cm.) in length become available in early summer. Pruning (when necessary) can also be done at this time. It is often early May before the leaf buds start to show, so do not think you have lost it, when it doesn't start its new growth till then.

Three-year-old plants need 24 inches (60 cm.) between them.

It is used in medicine and in the perfume industry. It can also be used in pot-pourris, but do not mix it with lavender.

Woodruff, Sweet *(Asperula odorata).* A hardy perennial plant, growing 8 to 10 inches (20 to 30 cm.) high. Complete shade is necessary, and a moist soil in which leaf mold has been well mixed.

It may be propagated by seed as soon as ripe, or by division of the whole plant. Although it spreads by underground shoots, for some reason these seldom "take" when replanted.

Plant your stock plants about 12 inches (30 cm.) apart, and do not disturb the bed for a couple of years. Under the benches in a lath house is an ideal situation for it.

It is used in medicine and in snuffs. Insects don't like it. It is also used to flavor wines and liqueurs, and is the Waldmeister used to make the Maibowle in Germany.

Only the dried Herb smells, not the fresh.

Wormwood *(Artemisia absinthium)*. A very hardy perennial, grow-ing about 48 inches (1.20 m.) high.

It thrives best in a poor, light soil; in heavy soil its silvery color tends to diminish. It likes full sun, but will tolerate some shade.

Propagation is by seed in spring; cuttings may also be taken.

Mature plants need to be 36 inches (90 cm.) apart.

It is used in medicine and in the liqueur industry. It is also an insecticide; moths dislike its smell.

SAFFRON CROCUS *(Crocus sativus)*

WHAT EACH OF THE 32 MORE HERBS
CAN BE USED FOR

Agrimony	Dyeing, medicine, tea
Alkanet	Dyeing
Basil, Bush	Insect repellent, flavor, medicine
Bay	Flavor, medicine
Bedstraw	Dyeing, flavor, medicine
Bergamot	Cosmetics, medicine, tea
Burnet, Salad	Flavor
Calendula	Dyeing, flavor, medicine
Chamomile, English or Roman	Beer, cosmetics, insect repellent, medicine, perfume
Chamomile, German	Bees, medicine, tea
Elecampane	Liqueurs, medicine
Horehound	Flavor, medicine
Hyssop	Bees, insect repellent, liqueurs, medicine, perfume
Lovage	Flavor, medicine, perfume, tea
Madder	Dyeing, medicine
Mints—Spear	Cosmetics, flavor, medicine, tea
Variegated Apple	Ornamental
Bergamot	Insect repellent, medicine, perfume, tea
Mullein	Dyeing, medicine
Pennyroyal	Insect repellent, medicine, tea
Pyrethrum	Insect repellent
Rose Geranium	Flavor, perfume
Rue	Cosmetics, insect repellent, medicine
Saffron Crocus	Dyeing, flavor, medicine
Santolina	Insect repellent, medicine, perfume
Sorrel, French	Flavor, vegetable
Southernwood	Insect repellent, medicine, ornamental
Tansy	Cosmetics, dyeing, flavor, insect repellent, liqueurs, medicine
Thymes (Various)	Bees, flavor, medicine, ornamental, perfume
Verbena, Lemon	Medicine, perfume, tea
Woodruff, Sweet	Insect repellent, liqueurs, medicine, and to flavor wine
Wormwood	Insect repellent, liqueurs, medicine

HYSSOP (*Hyssopus officinalis*)

HOW EACH OF THE 32 MORE HERBS
CAN BE USED

All the 32 more Herbs listed will be found
in at least one of the lists below.

Herbs for a Bee Garden

Chamomiles
Hyssop
Thymes (various)

*Herbs for Cosmetics
and/or Perfumes*

Bergamot
Chamomiles
Hyssop
Lovage
Mints—Spear
    Bergamot
Rose Geranium
Rue
Santolina
Tansy
Thymes (various)
Verbena, Lemon

*Herbs Used as
Sugar Savers*

None

Herbs Used for Teas

Agrimony
Bergamot
Chamomiles
Lovage
Mints—Spear
    Bergamot
Pennyroyal
Verbena, Lemon

An Ornamental Herb

Mint, Variegated Apple

Herbs for Dyes

Agrimony
Alkanet
Bedstraw
Calendula
Madder
Mullein
Saffron Crocus
Tansy

*Herbs Used
in Medicine*

Agrimony
Basil, Bush
Bay
Bedstraw
Bergamot
Calendula
Chamomiles
Elecampane
Horehound
Hyssop
Lovage
Madder
Mints—Spear
    Bergamot
Mullein
Pennyroyal
Rue
Saffron Crocus
Santolina
Southernwood
Tansy
Thymes (various)
Verbena, Lemon
Woodruff, Sweet
Wormwood

Herbs Used in Liqueurs

Elecampane
Hyssop
Tansy
Woodruff, Sweet
Wormwood

*Herbs for Flavor
and/or in the Kitchen*

Basil, Bush
Bay
Bedstraw
Burnet, Salad
Calendula
Horehound
Lovage
Mint, Spear
Rose Geranium
Saffron Crocus
Sorrel, French
Tansy
Thymes (various)
Woodruff, Sweet

*Herbs for
Repelling Insects*

Basil, Bush
Bergamot
Chamomiles
Hyssop
Pennyroyal
Pyrethrum
Rue
Santolina
Southernwood
Tansy
Woodruff, Sweet
Wormwood

PYRETHRUM (*Chrysanthemum cinerariaefolium*)

CHAPTER 10

Herb Products with Commercial Possibilities

Earlier chapters in this book have told you how to produce Herb plants, fresh cut Herbs, and fresh and dried plant material, and suggested possible outlets and markets for all these items.

This chapter will take you a step further, suggesting products you can make from fresh and dried Herbs. It is solely concerned with ideas, instructions, and recipes for making *salable* Herb products. No matter whether your skills and interests lie in the kitchen, with a sewing machine, or a needle and thread, or whether you have various artistic bents, there are ideas here which will be of use to you.

Culinary Products to Make with Fresh Herbs

HERB VINEGARS

Vinegars probably are the best known products which are flavored with fresh Herbs. Start with good quality vinegars whose acidity is not less than 5 percent and produce gourmet quality products. Use only red or white wine vinegar; the color depending on the Herb being used. Herb vinegars made with cider vinegar are also very palatable, but would not be considered gourmet products, so fetch a lower price. Of course, the cider vinegar would be cheaper to buy, but the work of producing either type is the same.

Get in touch with a wholesale grocer, and buy your wine vinegars from him. Purchase the minimum amount he will supply—and do your experimenting. Retail prices of wine vinegars are very high,

159

but your cider vinegar can be purchased retail for experimenting, as you would be unable to get it at wholesale in small enough quantities. White and malt vinegars are not suitable to use.

Herb vinegars can be made from any of the culinary Herbs, but some are a much better commercial proposition than others. These are listed in a chart at the end of this section, which also shows the part of the Herb to use, and the vinegar which seems to me gives the best results. It is unwise commercially to use more than one Herb to flavor a vinegar.

You will need glass jars for marinating the Herbs in the vinegar, and later, if you go into large-scale production, five- and/or ten-gallon stone crocks with covers. A pestle and mortar and/or a blender are also required.

Use simple bottles for the finished product, but have an attractive label. Also put a sprig of the Herb which gives its flavor to the vinegar in the bottle, and indicate on the label what type of vinegar has been used.

When it is necessary to boil the vinegar, use enamel or stainless steel saucepans—*never* use aluminum utensils. Some people recommend boiling all vinegar before use, even pouring it boiling on the Herb leaves, though I did not find this necessary.

How to make Herb vinegar from leaves. To each quart (4 cups) of vinegar, allow 2 cups of leaves of the selected Herb, which should be harvested at the peak of their flavor—see Chapter 4, "How and When to Harvest Herbs."

1. Blend the Herb leaves gently for a few seconds at lowest speed in the blender, or macerate them with a pestle and mortar.
2. Put the leaves into glass jars or crocks, and pour the vinegar (at room temperature) over them.
3. Stir daily. Stand for 10 days in a warm place.
4. Strain out the leaves through fine cheesecloth. Taste the vinegar. If it is not "herby" enough, repeat steps 1 to 4 with a fresh lot of Herb leaves.
5. Run through filter paper.
6. Pour into sterile bottles and cork securely.

How to make Herb vinegar from seeds. To each quart (4 cups) of vinegar allow 2 to 3 tablespoons of the selected seeds.

1. Bruise the seeds in a blender or pestle and mortar.
2. Put them in a glass jar.

3. Warm vinegar and pour onto the seeds.
4. Shake or stir daily. Stand for 10 to 14 days in a warm place.
5. Strain off the seeds, using cheesecloth.
6. Run the vinegar through filter paper.
7. Pour into sterile bottles and cork securely.

How to make Herb vinegar from roots. To each quart (4 cups) of vinegar allow ½ cup of grated root.

1. Grate or blend roots.
2. Bring vinegar to the boil.
3. Pour vinegar over the grated roots.
4. Repeat steps 4, 5, 6 and 7, as for making vinegar with seeds.

How to make Garlic vinegar. To each quart (4 cups) of vinegar allow six to eight cloves of Garlic.

1. Squash cloves with the *flat* of a large kitchen knife, but do not macerate them.
2. Pour vinegar (at room temperature) over the cloves and leave for 24 hours *only*.
3. Strain through filter paper.
4. Pour into sterile bottles and cork securely.

Note: Depending on the pungency of the Garlic, suggested quantities may give too strong or too weak a flavor. Adjust the amount of Garlic to your needs, but do *not* steep the cloves in the vinegar longer than 24 hours.

HERB VINEGARS

Herb to Use	Part of Herb	Vinegar to Use
Basil	Leaves	White wine
Burnet, Salad	Leaves	White wine
Dill	Seeds	Red wine
Fennel	Seeds	Red wine
Garlic	Cloves	Red Wine
Lovage	Root	Red wine
Marjoram, Sweet	Leaves	White wine
Mint, English	Leaves	Cider
Rosemary	Leaves	White wine
Sage	Leaves	Red wine
Tarragon, French	Leaves	White wine
Thyme, Garden	Leaves	White wine

HERB OILS

These are made with the same Herbs used for the Herb vinegars. Except in the case of Garlic, when the cloves are used, the leaves and any stems which are green and soft are macerated and marinated in a good-quality salad oil. Safflower oil is excellent and sunflower good also, but do not use an oil which has much taste of its own, for this could drown the flavor of the Herbs (except for Garlic!). Indicate on the label what oil has been used.

Once again, buy from a wholesale grocer after you have done your small-scale experimenting. Use wide-mouth glass containers for marinating the Herbs.

How to make Herb oils with leaves. To each pint (2 cups) of oil allow ½ cup of crushed or blended Herb.

1. Put Herbs and oil into a glass container (Mason jars are ideal), leaving an inch of space at the top.
2. Add 2 tablespoons of white wine vinegar.
3. Cover securely.
4. Stand in the sun for two or three weeks, and shake daily, *or* process as you would fruit juice in a hot water bath canner, every day for a week. This imitates the effect of the sun warming it and the night cooling it repeatedly day after day.
5. Strain off the oil, taste and smell. If it is not strong enough (there should be a strong odor of the Herb when you rub a little on your hand), repeat steps 1 through 4, and next time you make the oil, increase the proportions of crushed leaves to oil.

How to make Garlic oil. Follow the directions for making Garlic vinegar, using oil instead of vinegar, and half the amount of Garlic cloves.

FRENCH DRESSINGS AND MAYONNAISE

These can be made from standard recipes but using Herb vinegars and/or oils instead of unflavored ones.

HERB JELLIES

Use any apple jelly recipe, calculating the amount of the fresh Herb needed, based on these quantities. To every 3 cups of the apple

ROSE GERANIUM (*Pelargonium graveolens*)

juice, allow either 1 cup of English Mint leaves, or ¼ cup of Thyme leaves, or ¼ cup of Rosemary leaves, or 1 cup of Lemon Verbena or Lemon Balm leaves. Then follow your own apple jelly recipe, simmering the Herbs in the sugar and juice while the jelly is cooking. They must be strained out before putting up the jelly.

If you have no fresh Herbs available, use one-third or a quarter of the specified quantity in dried form.

Some Herbs seem to have an affinity for grape, orange, lemon, or grapefruit juices. Try these for something different. The amounts given below, using 4 cups of sugar, will "jell" with half a bottle or a 2 ounce packet of commercial pectin. Follow the manufacturer's directions for making the jelly, but allow:

> ¼ cup of Sweet Marjoram leaves to 3 cups of grapefruit juice
>
> or ½ cup of Rose Geranium leaves to ½ cup of lemon juice and 2½ of water
>
> or ½ cup of Rosemary leaves to 1½ cups water, ½ cup lemon and 1 cup of orange juice
>
> or ½ cup of Summer Savory leaves to 3 cups of grape or grapefruit juice
>
> or ¼ cup of Garden Thyme leaves to 3 cups of grape juice.

CANDIED OR CRYSTALLIZED HERBS

These are a delicate and time-consuming product to make, but the price you will get for them, if they are well-made and attractively packaged, will be very worthwhile.

How to candy or crystallize Angelica stems. Use tender young stems, cut early in the spring. Stems from a later, second cut can also be used, but the first spring cut is the best.

1. Cut the stems into four-inch lengths.
2. Simmer gently for a few minutes, until you can peel them easily.
3. Peel them, and boil again until they are tender and bright green.

4. Dry and weigh them. Allow one pound of sugar to one pound of stems.
5. Sprinkle sugar over the stems, and let them stand for two days.
6. Bring to the boil, straining off excess syrup. Measure syrup with a saccharimeter, and add enough sugar to bring it up to a 25-degree density.
7. Bring to the boil again and pour it over the stems; leave overnight.
8. The next day, pour off the syrup and check its density. Add sugar to bring it up to a 25-degree density again. Boil.
9. Pour over the stems once more. Repeat at intervals of 24 hours until the Angelica stems look semi-transparent, and no more sugar can be absorbed.
10. Spread out to dry in a warm place or near gentle heat.

How to candy or crystallize leaves and flowers. The most popular leaves will be from one of the Mints (except the Variegated Apple Mint), but by all means try other Herb leaves, too. Borage is an excellent flower to use, and, incidentally, crystallized violets and rose petals also are salable.

1. Gather the flowers or leaves when they are quite dry.
2. Dissolve 2 ounces of gum arabic in 1¼ cups of water (10 fluid ounces) in the top of a double boiler; then cool it.
3. Dip one leaf or one flower at a time into the cooled gum arabic. (Raw white of egg can also be used, but is not as satisfactory for commercial production.)
4. Spread out on a clean paper, and sprinkle with berry (fine granulated) sugar.
5. Dry for 24 hours.
6. Dissolve 2 cups of granulated sugar in 1¼ cups of water.
7. Heat to 240° F. (soft ball stage); keep the syrup well skimmed.
8. Cool.
9. Dip the flowers or leaves in, one by one, *or* pour the syrup over flowers or leaves, and leave them in the syrup for 24 hours.
10. Drain, sprinkle with berry sugar again, dry with gentle heat as in drying Herbs (see Chapter 5, "How to Dry Herbs").

How to candy roots. Lovage, Angelica, and Sweet Cicely roots can be candied, too.

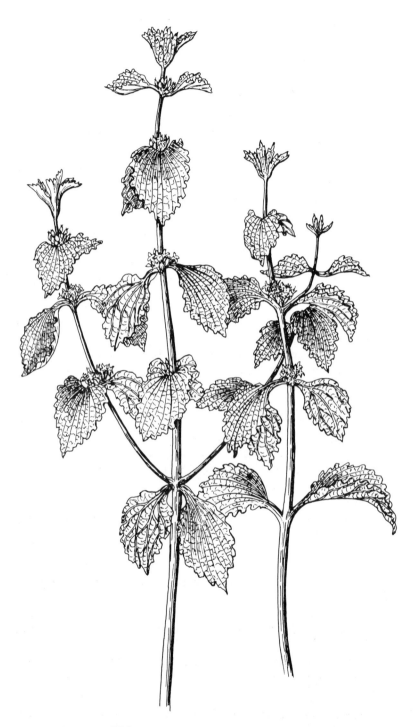

HOREHOUND (*Marubium vulgaris*)

1. Dig roots when the leaves have died down, at the end of the growing season.
2. Wash them with a hose gun.
3. Slice them very thinly.
4. Boil them in a small amount of water for half an hour.
5. Change the water and boil until they are tender. This may take an hour or more, depending on the toughness of the roots.
6. Make a syrup of ½ cup of water to every 2 cups of sugar.
7. Put in the drained roots, and boil till they are transparent.
8. Drain off the surplus syrup. Spread on waxed paper to dry, near gentle heat.
9. Pack attractively.

HERB SUGAR CANDIES

You will find the most popular flavors for Herb candies to be Peppermint, English Mint, Horehound, and Anise. Recipes using honey in place of sugar can be used—soft candy recipes, too. Use your imagination, a reliable candy recipe book, and the basic Herb recipe below.

BASIC RECIPE FOR MAKING HERB CANDIES

Put 4 cups of water in a saucepan, and add:

1 ½ cups of the leaves of the Herb chosen for flavor,

or

2 tablespoons full of seeds. Bring to the boil slowly, and simmer for 15 minutes. Strain off the Herb. Remove from heat. Add:
3 cups of granulated sugar and
3 cups of brown sugar. Stir till dissolved. Boil to a "hard crack," and remove from the heat. Pour into an oiled, shallow pan. Mark into squares as soon as possible. Break up as soon as it is hard. Wrap each piece in waxed or candy paper, and pack attractively.

SUGGESTED OUTLETS

Retail stores that might consider marketing your culinary products made with fresh Herbs are gourmet shops, delicatessens, and natural and health food stores. Items such as candied Herbs would be more suitable for gift shops to handle than natural and health food stores, as they contain so much sugar.

All these items could be sold from your farm (if you sell retail); they are also suitable mail order items. Remember that items with a limited shelf life should be date-stamped.

Culinary Products to Make
with Dried Herbs

PACKAGING DRIED CULINARY HERBS

Herbs for fragrant teas and for flavor in cooking can be dried and packaged separately—or blends of two or more Herbs can be made and packaged. Suggestions for marketing them are found under "Culinary Herbs" in Chapter 6.

For teas. Herbs to grow, dry, and package to make fragrant teas are: Angelica, Anise (seed), Bergamot, Catnip, English and German Chamomile, Dill (seed), Fennel (seed), Lemon Balm, Sweet Marjoram, Lovage, all the Mints (except the Variegated Apple Mint), Oregano, Pennyroyal, Rosemary, Sage, both Savories, Garden Thyme, Lemon Thyme, and Lemon Verbena.

For flavoring. Herbs to grow, dry and package for flavoring food are: Anise (seed), Bush and/or Sweet Basil, Bay, Caraway (seed), Coriander (seed), Dill (seed), Fennel (seed), Lemon Balm, Lovage (seed and leaves), Sweet Marjoram, English Mint, Peppermint, Spearmint, Oregano, Parsley (see Chapter 7 for special instructions for drying Parsley), Rosemary, both Sages, both Savories, French Tarragon, Garden and Lemon Thyme.

Blends of tea Herbs and Herbs for flavor can be made with combinations of two or more of these Herbs, but *great* care is needed in selecting them. Until you are very familiar with all of their tastes and smells, do not try to make and market your own blends. Start by checking the market to see what blends are popular. (See "Two Classic Blends of Herbs" in this chapter.) Commercial packages will indicate *which* Herbs their blends contain, though you may have to experiment to get the right proportions.

In Chapter 5 you will find the directions for harvesting, drying, preparing, and storing Herbs. So rub down or powder your Herbs for flavoring food, but keep the leaves of tea Herbs as whole as possible, as suggested.

Packaging. Packages of one and two ounces should be made up for the retail market. If you are supplying restaurants, half-pound sizes probably would be suitable, but consult the chefs as to their needs.

Packaging can be simple or elaborate, according to the market you are supplying. For instance, Herbs for flavor could be marketed in three types of containers for retail and mail order sales: plain plastic bags, glass containers with sprinkler tops for the powdered Herbs, and some handmade ceramic containers for the "gourmet" market. For your chefs, use inexpensive plastic bags.

Herbs for teas, being more bulky since they are not rubbed down or powdered, need larger containers for the same weight of Herbs. If you can get green-colored cellophane bags, they are not only inexpensive, but are much more attractive than plastic. Look in the Yellow Pages of your telephone directory to find wholesale container suppliers.

Labelling. Design a distinctive label to attach to all your products. It need not be elaborate, but it should be distinctive and should tie in with your operation. Check with your regional Food and Drug Administration office for regulations about labelling all food products.

TWO CLASSIC BLENDS OF HERBS

The most famous blends of culinary Herbs are "Les Fines Herbes" and "Bouquet Garni." Unfortunately the former is not suitable for use in dried form, since it consists of two parts Chervil and two parts Chives (neither of which retains much flavor when dried) to two parts Parsley and one part Tarragon. A window box of these four Herbs should be a good seller, however.

"Bouquet Garni" contains Sweet Bay, and, unless you live in a frost-free area, you will have difficulty in growing it on a commercial scale—so buy it from a wholesaler. The proportions are: 1 part Bay leaves, 12 parts Parsley and 4 parts Garden Thyme. Celery leaves can also be added to Bouquet Garni, though this is not essential.

Another way of measuring the blend is to allow one Bay leaf to
one tablespoon of Parsley, and one teaspoon of Garden Thyme. All
the Herbs should be rubbed very fine or powdered.

Visit your public library and study cook books—not only the
American and English, but Continental ones as well. Experiment
with combinations taken from these books and also see what new
ideas *you* can come up with.

HERB SALTS FOR FLAVOR

Blends of Herbs, or any of the individual culinary Herbs, can be
powdered and mixed with an equal amount (by volume) of table or
sea salt, for packaging in a small container with a sprinkler top.
These are used in the kitchen and at the table instead of ordinary
salt, being especially good on salads.

BAKED GOODS

Yeast breads, soda breads, cookies, and plain cakes can all be
flavored with dried powdered Herbs. Use your own favorite recipes
and allow ¾ to 1 teaspoon of the powdered Herb to each cup of
sifted flour. If you are using seeds, crush them and add one teaspoon to each cup of flour. This is just to give you a guide to start.
After a few trials, you may like to increase or decrease the quantities
of some of the Herbs.

There are some excellent natural food recipe books on the market,
which include many recipes for baked goods with Herb flavoring,
and some standard cook books include recipes with Herbs, too.

SUGGESTED OUTLETS

Retail outlets which might consider marketing your culinary Herb
products made with dried Herbs are gourmet shops, delicatessens,
and natural and health food stores. You could also sell these products direct from your farm (if you retail) and all of them except the
baked goods could be sold by mail order. Remember that the baked
goods have a limited shelf life so the best way to start in this area
would be to bake for special orders only.

LOVAGE (*Levisticum officinalis*)

Perfumed Products to Make
with Fresh Herbs

HERBAL WREATHS

Whether you can make Herbal wreaths for Christmas depends on
your winter climate; but whatever your climate, you will be able to
make them from late spring to early fall. Use the woody perennial
evergreen Herbs—Rosemary, Winter Savory, and the bushy
Thymes will be the longest-lasting. You can use a styrofoam, or a
moss and wire wreath base, though the latter can be kept damp and
will last longer.

TUSSIE MUSSIES

These are attractive little nosegays of Herbs, or Herbs and flowers.
Originally they were carried by judges in eighteenth-century En-
gland to ward off the smells in their courts! They are most suitable
for Valentine's Day, especially since special sentiments can be
expressed according to the "language of flowers."

Often a Rose bud is placed at the center. It can be surrounded
with a few gray-green leaves, such as Santolina, a few sprigs of
Rosemary, and then Mint leaves or Lemon Balm. The whole should
be strongly tied with thread. They can be sold fresh, and later hung
to dry. In that way they will retain their scent for a long time.

SUGGESTED OUTLETS

Herbal wreaths and Tussie Mussies should be marketed through
gift shops, florist shops and by direct sales from your farm (if you
retail). They are not suitable for mail order.

Perfumed Products to Make
with Dried Herbs

POT-POURRI

"Dry" pot-pourri can be made from well-dried fragrant flowers and leaves, the "Wet" pot-pourri from the same ingredients dried only enough to give them a leathery consistency. Spices and essential oils often are added to both types.

Before you go into this field commercially, you should study the subject thoroughly.

Most pot-pourri recipes call for scented rose petals, so you will need a source of these. Here is a short list of some of the roses grown for their perfume:

1. *Rosa damascena* or "Damask Rose," and its hybrids.
2. *Rose gallica,* or "Provins Rose," and its hybrids.
3. "Eugene Furst," "Hugh Dickson," "General Jacqueminot," "Ulrich Brünner," "Richmond," and "Liberty." These last are all hybrid perpetuals.

However, if you just want to make a simple *Herb* pot-pourri, you can do this by mixing any of the following dried Herb leaves and/or flowers:

Angelica, Basil, Borage flowers, Lemon Balm, Lemon Verbena, Lovage, Sweet Marjoram, various Mints (use only one kind in each mix), Rosemary, Sage, Garden or Lemon Thyme, and, of course, Lavender—which mixes well with any of the other Herbs except the lemon-scented ones.

HERB PILLOWS

Nobody can deny that Herb-scented pillows are pleasant and soothing things to lay one's head on. Some people find that they are sleep-inducing too. They can be made with a simple cotton cover, or you can make elaborate and beautiful covers with prints, sheers, hand-embroidered or hand-woven cases, in all kinds of colors, shapes, and sizes. The one essential to remember is to have the inner case (in which you put the crushed, dried Herbs) of a fine enough weave to prevent them from leaking out!

Herbs suitable for use in these pillows are a matter of personal taste. But to guide you, here are a few suggestions.

Use equal quantities of dried:

> Lavender flowers, Peppermint and Angelica leaves
> or Lemon Verbena, English Mint, and Sweet Marjoram leaves
> or Lemon Balm, Peppermint, and Angelica leaves
> or Rosemary and Rose Geranium leaves
> or Lavender flowers, Thyme and Rose Geranium leaves
> or Sage, Peppermint, and Lemon Balm leaves.

Lavender, some of the Mints, Lemon Thyme, Lemon Balm, or Lemon Verbena, can each be used alone. Any mix you make for pot-pourri can also be used.

A word of warning: Some books suggest that you use a fixative, but beware of Orris root powder. Some people are very allergic to it.

HERB SACHETS

Sachets can be made in a great variety of materials, but should be smaller than the Herb pillows. They are used to perfume drawers and cupboards, thin, flat ones being particularly useful to lay amongst clean household linen. Use any Herb or Herb mixture listed under "Herb Pillows."

MOTH PREVENTATIVES

The sweetest smelling of the Herbs for discouraging moths are Lavender, Rosemary, Garden and Lemon Thymes, and the Mints. Even more effective are Santolina, Southernwood, Tansy, and Wormwood.

Their dried leaves can be made into sachets and bags filled with one or a combination of the suggested Herbs, to hang on hangers.

HAIR RINSES

Package ½ cup of Rosemary leaves in a cheesecloth bag, with instructions to add 2½ cups of boiling water to it, and when it is cool, to use it as a hair rinse for dark hair.

For fair hair, package ½ cup of Chamomile flowers (either German or English) with similar instructions.

BATH PERFUMES

Herbs which seem to have the most appeal for perfuming the bath are Angelica, Basil, Chamomile flowers, Lavender, Lemon Balm and Lemon Verbena, Lovage (which is a deodorant), any of the Mints, Pennyroyal, Rosemary, Sage, and any of the Thymes. Make up combinations of several of these Herbs, putting them into cheesecloth bags large enough to hold one cup of crushed (not powdered) dried Herb leaves. These bags can be sold individually or in gift boxes, and can be made up of six or twelve bags with a variety of fragrances. Of course you can make bags of any one Herb, but the combinations are much more interesting.

HERBAL AIR FRESHENERS

The leaves of Lavender, Lemon Balm, Lovage, Sweet Marjoram, Rosemary, Rue, Sage, Santolina, Southernwood, Tansy, and Garden and Lemon Thymes, make good air fresheners when burnt in powdered form. The Herbs can be packaged individually or in mixes. Several varieties boxed with a little incense burner make an unusual gift item.

HERB-SCENTED STATIONERY

Any of the sweet-scented Herbs can be used to decorate and perfume note paper, greeting, and Christmas cards.

A slit can be made in the back of a card, and a sprig of dried Herb inserted into it, or a tiny bag of dried Herb can be attached to the

SANTOLINA or LAVENDER COTTON
(*Santolina chamaecyparissus*)

card. Boxes of stationery can be decorated with pressed, dried Herb leaves or flowers, and a little bag of the same dried Herb placed in the box to perfume the paper and envelopes.

CATNIP TOYS

The Catnip toy market is big business, but is only worth going into if you are willing to take the time and trouble to produce first-class dried Catnip, and with the use of good-quality materials, make toys with a professional finish. Package them with care and originality, for you will have many competitors in this field.

Your finished toy must have "nose appeal" for the cats, and "eye appeal" for the customers, so you will need to:

1. Grow your Catnip plants in a well-drained and sunny spot; preferably where the soil is light and sandy. See also Chapter 3, List D.
2. Harvest it as the flower buds are starting to open.
3. Dry it with care and gentle warmth (see Chapter 5 for harvesting and drying instructions).
4. Rub the leaves off the stems, being careful not to powder them. Then you will need:
5. A tough fabric with a firm weave, which will stand up to cats' sharp claws and teeth. Make a few toys, and let your cats and your friends' cats test the toughness of several different materials—before you go into large-scale production. You will soon find out which are the toughest!
6. A sewing machine and the usual sewing accessories, including a pair of sharp scissors.
7. Bags and/or boxes for packaging the toys. These should have bright, eye-catching illustrations on them. Be original with your designs.

Decide what shape the toys will be. Catnip mice are traditional—but a lot of work. Make them 3 inches long and 2 inches high. Strings of Catnip sausages would be original. Make each sausage about 3 inches long and a half inch thick. Have three or four in each string. Catnip fish can be made in many different shapes and sizes.

If all these toys are too difficult for you to make, Catnip sachets, 2 by 4 inches, are simple to make and just as acceptable to cats. None of the toys should weigh more than one ounce, and if you want to make a size for kittens, it should weigh only half an ounce.

SUGGESTED OUTLETS

Retail outlets which might consider marketing all your perfumed products made with dried Herbs are gift shops, florists, natural and health food stores. You can sell them directly from the farm (if you retail), and they are good items to sell by mail order. The Catnip toys can also be retailed through pet shops.

Some Points to Remember

- ◆ The right name for your farm or garden helps people to remember you. Take time and thought to find a really distinctive name.
- ◆ Consistently good quality is a *must*.
- ◆ Trouble taken over the appearance of any product is never wasted.
- ◆ If you have made a promise to deliver, keep it, however inconvenient to you.
- ◆ A phone call to a customer, if arrangements are *unavoidably* altered, should be made in time for him to remake *his* plans. (This applies especially when deliveries to restaurants are being made.)
- ◆ The knowledge that customers can rely on you builds confidence and good business relationships. Make every effort not to let them down.
- ◆ You cannot afford to "carry" accounts for anybody. Try to arrange for cash-on-delivery. Only run monthly accounts if you make large sales to big firms. Have a chat with the accounts department as soon as you make your first delivery.
- ◆ If you want to sell by mail order, a small advertisement in a nationally read garden magazine, though expensive, will bring you to the notice of many interested people who otherwise

would never have heard of you. On the other hand, if your sales are to be from the farm, local advertising will be more useful. Place a small advertisement regularly in your local newspaper, posters in your retail outlets, have business cards, a modest catalog of the plants and products you have for sale, and distinctive labels on all orders sent out. This is enough for your first few years. (We found that publicity from newspaper articles, national weekly papers, and even local T.V. shows, was very short-lived and disappointing.)

🌢 Local and national health, agricultural, and horticultural regulations are there for your and your customer's benefit. Comply with them.

🌢 You must not make claims for the curative properties of your Herbs (no matter what you know they will do). You may say that a certain Herb is "reputed" to relieve this or that symptom—but no more.

🌢 There are advantages in being classified as a farmer for income tax purposes. (You can obtain the free "Farmer's Tax Guide," from the Internal Revenue Service or County Extension Agent.)

If you receive two-thirds of your gross income from the sale of plants, nursery stock and/or garden produce, you are a "farmer." So keep accurate records of costs, purchases, sales, labor, etc., to see if you can classify as a farmer. Your Extension Service will help you with information and advice.

🌢 You should keep a garden diary, recording all you do each day (which doesn't take as long as you would think). As well as this diary, a large-scale plan of the garden should be put up in the potting shed or greenhouse, and on it carefully record the date and the work as it is done. Put down what goes into each bed—fertilizers, compost, plants, etc. This record is essential when planning future planting, and is useful for reference over the years.

🌢 Until you are very well established, keep your operation small enough not to need paid help. The day may come when you find that you have more work than two people can handle. Then you will have to make a choice: Whether you want to start employing labor, or would find it better to specialize in fewer fields and cut out production in areas which are less profitable. Your well-kept records will be invaluable to help you decide what to cut out, and what to continue to produce—and perhaps increase.

🐍 Empty bench space in the greenhouse (except in hot summer weather) represents a loss of income. Try to plan your output so that as one batch of plants is ready to go (either for sale or to be hardened off in the lath house), another is ready to fill the spaces on the benches—either seedlings just pricked out, or cuttings just potted up. It will take a year or two to do this efficiently, and it is yet another reason to keep accurate records of all you do.

🐍 You also should keep records of all the things you were asked for, but were unable to supply.

🐍 Two or three people, however, don't make a profitable market for a new product. It often seems that several people will ask within a few days for something that you do not have, and you will be left wondering if it might not be worth starting production of that item. Be cautious, especially if it entails laying out cash or much time (which is also money).

On the other hand, because a certain Herb has not sold for a year or two does not mean that it never will. Keep a few stock plants, even if you stop propagating. The week after you dig up that non-selling Herb and throw it on the compost heap, somebody will ask for it!

🐍 You will find ways to short-cut routine work as you get more experienced. If a new job means endless labor, look for ways to streamline your techniques. This is especially important when you are mass-producing plants.

🐍 Some Herbs are in great demand and/or short supply—especially French Tarragon. Do not sell *one single plant* until you have built up a really large bed of propagating stock. Resist those persuasive customers. Make them wait! One plant sold to them this year would have made five or six more stock plants by next year.

🐍 A sense of humor can be a great asset when dealing with the public. There is always the old customer who comes back with a friend, and stops her from buying a plant from you because "I have plenty in my garden. I'll give you a bit." And another customer says, "How expensive; it grows from seed." Asked why she doesn't try growing her own, she will probably confess that she couldn't get the seed to germinate!

🐍 Most people are honest, but if you prefer not to accept checks when you are retailing from the farm, put up a polite sign: "Sorry, we cannot accept personal checks." There may be the occasional customer who you will feel badly about refusing, and

MADDER (*Rubia tinctorum*)

you may even lose a sale or two. However, this way you will not have losses from bad checks — and these can mount up!

🪱 The greenhouse is not the place for customers. Their clothes may brush and damage plants, and some of them will handle plants, which is undesirable. Small children have been known to remove plant labels — even to change them around!

You may have stock plants not on your selling list, and, believe it or not, some people *will* take a cutting when your back is turned. You may not want to reveal some of your methods and other secrets, either.

Finally, there is a risk of disease being brought in. Does this sound ridiculous? We once had a customer who asked what was the matter with a Geranium stem, which she produced out of her pocket and threw on the bench amongst our newly imported scented geraniums! Just thoughtlessness, but it happened that her geranium had a virus disease which could have wiped out all of ours. So put a "No Admittance" sign on your greenhouse door! You always can make an exception if you want to.

🪱 The popular belief that "Herbs" are a strange and mystical group, different from all other plants yet similar to each other, is quite incorrect. Herbs come from a number of different botanical families (also called *natural orders*) which are entirely dissimilar. This is a great advantage, since it means that Herb-farming is not monoculture. In a very dry year you may have some poor crops, or even lose some Herbs. For instance, Mints love cool damp weather, and thrive in heat only where plenty of water is available. Thymes, on the other hand, will thrive in a hot, dry summer, with a minimum of irrigation. Conversely, in a very damp summer your Mints will thrive but your Thymes and Tarragon may suffer.

🪱 Many Herbs have close relatives which are common vegetables and flowers. Belonging to the *Umbelliferae* family are Parsley, Caraway, Chervil, Coriander, Dill, Fennel, Lovage, and Sweet Cicely, as well as Carrots, Parsnips and Queen Anne's Lace. In the *Labiatae* family are Basil, Catnip, Lemon Balm, the Marjorams and Mints, and many more Herbs; so are Stinging Nettles, both wild and cultivated, Coleus, Ground Ivy and Self-heal. Mullein belongs to the *Scrophulariaceae* family, and so does the Snapdragon and Toadflax.

🪱 It is important to identify all your plants by their Latin names. This is *not* affectation, as one lady suggested to me. Plants often have several common names, and conversely the *same* common name is often used for different plants.

The common garden "Geranium" for instance, is not a Geranium at all! Its Latin name is *Pelargonium grandiflorum*. However, the Meadow Cranesbill is (in Latin) *Geranium pratense*. There are three plants called Crowfoot, four called Pigweed, and three called Snakeweed, each belonging to different genera, and so having completely different Latin names!

Heliotropus peruviana is the Latin name for Heliotrope, which is also called Cherry Pie; but "Cherry Pie" is also used for the Great Hairy Willow Herb *(Epilobium hirsutum)*. In case you are not completely confused by now, let me tell you that there also is a variety of Petunia called Cherry Pie.

Do you see the need for Latin names now?

- Growing seed for sale is not for you. The machinery needed is expensive, and only large-scale production would warrant its purchase. If you want to sow some of your own seed, that's fine, but don't sell it for planting. Most countries have very strict regulations and standards, which a small grower cannot possibly meet.

  This does not refer, of course, to seed such as Anise, Coriander, Caraway, Dill, Fennel, Lovage, Sweet Cicely, when they are to be used in the kitchen for flavoring.

- You will get some marvelous ideas from glossy magazines and beautiful (but often unpractical) books. It may be fun to make a few of these pictured Herb articles, but beware of wasting time making unsalable products. For many years you will have little time to spare from commercial production.

- Except for a few shrubs and bulbs, cut out all ornamental flower beds (the exception to this is your formal Herb garden).

- It is worth the time and trouble of keeping grass cut short. It doesn't have to be a perfect lawn to be attractive, and is preferable to ill-kept flower beds.

- You should leave a little space in your planning to grow a few vegetables and some fruit. But a good motto, at least for the first few years, is: *If you can't sell it or eat it, don't grow it.*

SOUTHERNWOOD or OLD MAN (*Artemisia abrotanum*)

Glossary

Annual
A plant that is raised from seed and completes its growing cycle within one year (not necessarily a calendar year); flowering, fruiting and then dying.

Asexual
Reproduction without the union of male and female germ cells.

Biennial
A plant which grows from seed one year, from the roots the next, then seeding and dying, thus taking two years to complete its growing cycle.

Bolt
A plant is said to *bolt* when it produces seed prematurely. This sometimes occurs in very hot, dry weather.

Botanical family
A group of related genera (see genus) with a family resemblance, but distinct from each other.

Botanical name
The Latin name of a plant, usually consisting of two parts: first the genus, then the species.

Bud
An undeveloped stem or branch; an unexpanded flower.

Bulb
A modified bud, with fleshy leaf bases underground, which act as storage organs, enabling the plant to survive the winter. Often applied to plants with fleshy rootstocks, including corms and rhizomes.

Bushel (U.S.)
A unit of volume used in dry measures, equal to 4 pecks (2150.42 cubic inches).

185

Cambium Layer	A layer of cells between wood and bark, from which new wood and bark will grow.
Clove	One of the small wedge shaped bulblets which develop within a larger bulb.
Cold Frame	A wooden or aluminum frame with removable glass lights, in which plants can be protected from inclement weather, and in which they can be "hardened off."
Come True	A plant is said to "come true" when it is an exact replica of its parent plant.
Corm	A swollen underground stem, which sends out roots from its lower surface; it is bulb-like but solid.
Corolla	A collective name for the petals of a flower, whether they are separate or united.
Cotyledons	One of the primary leaves of an embryo plant, though the word is used for the first or "seed leaves," to distinguish them from the "true," or adult leaves. When the cotyledons are fully developed, and before the first "true" leaves appear, is the best time to prick out the seedlings, as roots are smaller and will be damaged less.
Cut Back or **Pinch Back**	To remove the growing tips and top parts of the stems, to encourage the plant to grow more bushy. Done when the plant is older and woody, it is necessary to use secateurs.
Decocoction	An extract made by boiling parts of the Herb (usually the root, bark, or seeds) in water.
Decumbent	Reclining, but with the tip growing upwards.
Dibber	A tool used for making holes in soil, into which seeds, seedlings or cuttings may be inserted.
Droop	To hang down, to become limp, usually from excessive heat and/or lack of water.
Friable	Easy to crumble.

SORREL, FRENCH (*Rumex scutatus*)

187

Genus   A term used to indicate a group of plants that may have a common ancestor and are similar in structure.

Germination   The earliest stage in the development of a seed.

Harden Off   The gradual exposing of plants, which have been raised under artificial conditions, to natural outdoor conditions.

Heel   The strip of bark, or wood, which comes off the main shoot when a cutting is pulled, rather than cut off a plant. Some cuttings seem to root more readily with this "heel" left on.

Herb   Botanically speaking, a plant without a permanent woody stem; but can also be used to denote plants of which some part can be used for their flavor, aromatic, or medicinal properties. According to Webster's *New World Dictionary* it may be pronounced either *Herb* or *érb*, that is, with the *H* either sounded or not.

Hybrid   The result of a cross between two parent plants which are dissimilar.

Infusion   An extract made by pouring boiling water over the leaves of Herbs; usually about ½ ounce of the leaves to a pint (2 cups) of water, allowing it to stand 10 to 15 minutes before straining.

Leaf Bud   An undeveloped leaf.

Macerate   To extract the constituents from Herbs by steeping them in water at room temperature for several hours, *or* to soften or separate by soaking, *or* to chop small.

Marinate   To steep in a flavored pickling solution.

Nip Off   To remove the growing tip of a plant, usually done with a finger and thumbnail while the plant is still soft and young.

Node   The point at which the leaf or leaf buds are attached to the stem of a plant.

Ovary   The ovule-bearing part of the pistle.

Ovule   The body that, after fertilization, becomes the seed.

Peck   A unit of volume used in dry measures, equal to 8 U.S. quarts (537.605 cubic inches).

Perennial   A plant having a life cycle of more than two seasons.

Petal   One of the separate divisions of the corolla.

Pinch Back See *Cut Back*.

Pistle   The seed-bearing organ of the flower, which usually consists of a *stigma, style,* and *ovary*.

Potbound or **Rootbound**   A condition which develops when a plant is left too long in a pot. The pot becomes too small for it and the roots become cramped, so that they are unable to develop further. A plant put into the garden in this condition will seldom develop, and usually remains stunted. Occasionally it is possible to disentangle the roots, to trim them, and then to plant them out, but NEVER sell plants in this condition.

Potting On When plants are beginning to get too large for their containers, they should be "potted on" into larger ones. This will avoid their becoming "potbound" or "rootbound" (see above).

Prick Out   To transplant seedlings from the container in which they were originally sown to the flat or pots in which they will have more room to develop, prior to planting out in the garden or selling.

Puddle In   When planting out plants from pots into the garden, a hole is made only slightly bigger than the plant pot; the hole is filled with water or liquid fertilizer solution and allowed to drain away. Then the plant is removed from its pot, put in the wet hole, and the soil is gently packed around it.

Ram, Hydraulic   A device for pumping water by means of water power, using the force of falling water to compress air rather than to turn a wheel.

Rhizomes	An underground stem or root stock. It may be a storage organ, enabling the plant to overwinter successfully.
Rootbound	See *Potbound*.
Root Stock	An underground part of the stem of some perennial Herbs, from which new shoots and roots grow each season.
Rub Down	To remove the leaves from the stems of dried Herbs, by gently rubbing them between the palms of the hands.
Runners	A slender trailing stem, taking root at the nodes.
Seed	A ripened ovule which contains the embryonic plant.
Species	A group of individual plants all belonging to the same genus.
Spices	Aromatic vegetable substances, grown in tropical and sub-tropical climates, that are often used to flavor food.
Stigma	The part of the pistle which receives the pollen.
Stratification	This is a process by which seeds are placed in moist sand or peat moss, and exposed to temperatures of 34° to 43° F. (1° to 6° C.) for several months.
Style	The narrow part of the pistle which connects the ovary and stigma.
Tap Root	A primary root growing downwards, from which small branch roots may develop.
Thinning Out	The removal of excessive seedlings, caused by too thickly sown seed. It should be done as early as possible in the plant's life, to avoid disturbing the roots of the plants which are to remain. It can be done in two stages, e.g., if plants are to stand eight inches apart, the first thinning out should leave a plant every four inches. Later, as they begin to touch, a final thinning can be done.

Vegetative   Propagation by asexual means.
  Propagation

Whorl   A circle of leaves arranged around the stem.

Wilt   To become limp from heat and/or lack of water.

THYMES, Various (*Thymus species*)

Appendix A

Quick-Reference Chart of 64 Herbs and Their Cultural Requirements

(Full cultural details are listed in Chapters 3 and 9)

	Life Span/ Hardiness	Height (Inches)	Soil	Light Saturation	Distance Apart, (Inches)
Agrimony	P H	24–36	Well drained, ordinary	Some shade	10
Alkanet	P H	24	Well drained, light sandy	Some sun	18
Angelica	B H	84	Moist rich	Part shade	36
Anise	A T	24	Ordinary	Full sun	4
Basil, Bush	A T	8	Well drained, rich	Full sun	12
Basil, Sweet	A T	18	Rich	Full sun	12
Bay	P T	240	Well drained, ordinary	Full sun	—
Bedstraw	P H	36	Dry sandy	Full sun	24
Bergamot	P H	36	Ordinary moist	Full sun or part shade	18
Borage	A H	36	Well drained, ordinary	Sun or part shade	18
Burnet, Salad	P H	18	Dry ordinary	Full sun	12

Explanation of abbreviations used:
A—Annual
B—Biennial
H—Hardy
P—Perennial
T—Tender

	Life Span/ Hardiness	Height (Inches)	Soil	Light Saturation	Distance Apart, (Inches)
Calendula	A H	24	Well drained, light sandy	Full sun	12
Caraway	B H	24	Ordinary	Full sun	8
Catnip	P H	36	Sandy dry	Full sun	18
Chamomile, English or Roman	P H	12	Well drained, light	Full sun	6
Chamomile, German	A H	24	Well drained, sandy	Full sun	8
Chervil	A H	6	Well drained, ordinary	Some shade	8
Chives	P H	8–12	Rich	Full sun	8
Comfrey	P H	24–36	Well manured, heavy	Full sun	36
Coriander	A H	24–36	Ordinary	Full sun	4
Dill	A H	36	Light sandy	Sheltered, full sun	10
Elecampane	P H	96	Moist light	Full sun	30
Fennel	P H	60	Well limed	Full sun	18
Garlic	P H	12	Well drained, rich	Full sun	6
Garlic Chives	P H	30	Rich	Full sun	10
Horehound	P H	24	Well drained, light sandy	Full sun or part shade	10
Hyssop	P H	18	Well drained, light	Full sun or part shade	12
Lavender, Tall	P H	30	Well drained, light	Full sun	36
Lavender, Dwarf	P H	12–18	Well drained, light	Full sun	24
Lemon Balm	P H	48	Well drained, sandy	Full sun or part shade	18
Lovage	P H	72–84	Moist rich	Some shade	36
Madder	P H	48 (De-cumbent)	Well drained, sandy	Full sun	10
Marjoram, Sweet	P T	9–12	Rich light	Full sun sheltered	12
Mints	P H	36	Rich moist	Full sun or some shade	18
Mullein	B H	96	Poor dry	Full sun or shade	18–24
Oregano	P H	18	Light dry	Full sun	18

	Life Span/ Hardiness		Height (Inches)	Soil	Light Saturation	Distance Apart, (Inches)
Parsley	B	H	8–12	Rich	Full sun or part shade	8
Pennyroyal	P	H	Prostrate	Moist heavy	Part shade	6
Pyrethrum	P	H	18–24	Well drained, limed	Full sun	18
Rose Geranium	P	T	36	Well drained, light	Full sun	36
Rosemary	P	H/T	48–60	Well drained, light	Full sun	36
Rue	P	H	24	Well drained, poor	Full sun or part shade	24
Saffron Crocus	P	H	3	Rich, well drained	Full sun or part shade	6
Sage Broad Leaf	P	H	18	Sandy limed	Full sun	24
Sage Narrow Leaf	P	H	18	Sandy limed	Full sun	24
Santolina	P	H	24	Light, well drained	Full sun	36
Savory, Summer	A	H	18	Light rich	Full sun	8
Savory, Winter	P	H	8	Poor, well drained	Full sun	12
Shallots	P	H	15	Rich, well drained	Full sun	8
Sorrel	P	H	30	Rich moist	Full sun	18
Southernwood	P	H	36	Ordinary	Full sun	48
Sweet Cicely	P	H	24	Rich moist	Part shade	24
Tansy	P	H	36	Ordinary, well drained	Full sun	48
Tarragon, French	P	H	24	Well drained, light	Full sun	12
Thyme, Garden	P	H	10	Sandy, well drained	Full sun	12
Thyme, Lemon	P	H	12	Sandy, well drained	Full sun	18
Thyme, *Serpyllum*	P	H	Low Creeping	Sandy, Well drained	Full sun	4
Thyme, *Barona*	P	H	Semi-Prostrate	Sandy, well drained	Full sun	8–12
Verbena, Lemon	P	T	Up to 96	Light, well drained	Full sun	24–36
Woodruff, Sweet	P	H	8–10	Moist leafy	Full shade	12
Wormwood	P	H	48	Poor light	Full sun or part shade	36

CHAMOMILE, GERMAN (*Matricaria chamomilla*)

Appendix B

Propagation and Pots

Method of propagation recommended to produce saleable plants *most quickly,* **and size of pots in which to plant rooted material**

Herb	Method of Propagation	Size Pot (Inches Square)
Agrimony	Root cuttings	4
Alkanet	Root cuttings	4
Angelica	Seed	4
Anise	Seed	3
Basil, Bush	Seed	3
Basil, Sweet	Seed	3
Bay	Stem cuttings	3
Bedstraw	Division	3
Bergamots	Division	4
Borage	Seed	3 or 4
Burnet, Salad	Seed	3
Calendula	Seed	3
Caraway	Seed	3
Catnip	Cuttings, or transplant self-sown seedlings	3 or 4
Chamomile, English or Roman	Division	3
Chamomile, German	Seed	3
Chervil	Seed	3
Chives	Division	4

Herb	Method of Propagation	Size Pot (Inches Square)
Comfrey	Root cuttings	4 or 5
Coriander	Seed	3
Dill	Seed	3
Elecampane	Root cuttings	4 or 5
Fennel, Sweet	Seed	4
Garlic	Not practical to sell plants	
Garlic Chives	Division	4
Horehound	Division	3 or 4
Hyssop	Stem cuttings	3
Lavender, Tall	Stem cuttings	3 or 4
Lavender, Dwarf	Stem cuttings	3
" "	Division	Field grow
Lemon Balm	Division, or transplant self-sown seedlings	3 or 4
Lovage	Division	4 or 5
Madder	Division	3 or 4
Marjoram, Sweet	Stem cuttings	3
Mints, All	Runners	4 or 5
Mullein	Seed, or transplant *small* self-sown seedlings	4 or 5
Oregano	Division	3 or 4
Parsley	Seed	2¼ tall
Pennyroyal	Runners	3
Pyrethrum	Division	3 or 4
Rose Geranium	Stem cuttings	3 or 4
Rosemary	Stem cuttings	3
Rue	Stem cuttings	3
Saffron Crocus	Corms	3
Sage, Broad leaf	Stem cuttings	4
Sage, Narrow leaf	Stem cuttings	4
Santolina	Stem cuttings	3
Savory, Summer	Seed	3
Savory, Winter	Stem cuttings, Plantlets from stool layering	3 3 or 4

Herb	Method of Propagation	Size Pot (Inches Square)
Shallots	Not practical to sell plants	
Sorrel	Seed	4
Southernwood	Stem cuttings	3
Sweet Cicely	Root cuttings	4 or 5
Tansy	Division	4 or 5
Tarragon, French	Division	3 or 4
Thyme, Garden	Stem cuttings	3
	Plantlets from stool-layering	4
Thyme, Lemon	Stem cuttings	3
	Plantlets from stool-layering	4
Thyme, *Serpyllum Barona*	Division	3
	Tip rooted branches can be cut off and replanted	3
Various	Division	3
Verbena, Lemon	Stem cuttings	3
Woodruff, Sweet	Division	3
Wormwood	Stem cuttings	4

WOODRUFF, SWEET (*Asperula odorata*)

Appendix C

Part of Herb to Harvest for Selling Fresh, for Drying, and for Packaging

Herb	Part to Harvest When Selling the Herb Fresh	Part to Harvest for Drying	Part to Package or Process for Selling Dried
Agrimony	Stems, leaves	Stems, leaves	Stems, leaves
Alkanet	Roots	Roots	Roots
Angelica	Stems	Leaves, stems, Seeds, roots	Leaves
Anise	—	Stems, leaves, Seeds	Leaves, seeds
Basil, Bush	Stems, leaves	Stems, leaves	Young stems, leaves
Basil, Sweet	Stems, leaves	Stems, leaves	Young stems, leaves
Bay	Leaves	Leaves	Leaves
Bedstraw	Roots	Roots	Roots
Bergamots	Stems, leaves	Stems, leaves	Leaves
Borage	Flowers	Flowers, leaves	Flowers, leaves
Burnet, Salad	Stems, leaves	Stems, leaves	Leaves
Calendula	Flowers	Flowers	Petals
Caraway	—	Seeds	Seeds
Catnip	Stems, leaves	Stems, leaves	Leaves
Chamomile, English or Roman	Flower heads	Flower heads	Flower heads
Chamomile, German	Flower heads	Flower heads	Flower heads
Chervil	Stems, leaves	Not Worth Drying	
Chives	Leaves	Not Worth Drying	

Herb	Part to Harvest When Selling the Herb Fresh	Part to Harvest for Drying	Part to Package or Process for Selling Dried
Comfrey	Leaves	Leaves, Stems, Roots (Better to use Fresh— Also is difficult to dry well)	Leaves, roots
Coriander	—	Seeds	Seeds
Dill	Stems, leaves	Seeds	Seeds
Elecampane	Roots	Roots	Roots
Fennel, Sweet	Stems, leaves	Seeds	Seeds
Garlic	Cloves	Cloves	Cloves
Garlic Chives	Leaves	Not Worth Drying	
Horehound	Stems, leaves	Stems, leaves	Leaves
Hyssop	Stems, leaves	Stems, leaves	Leaves
Lavender, Tall	Flowers, stalks	Flowers	Flowers
Lavender, Dwarf	Flowers, stalks	Flowers	Flowers
Lemon Balm	Stems, leaves	Stems, leaves	Leaves
Lovage	Stems, leaves	Stems, leaves	Stems, leaves
Madder	Roots	Roots	Roots
Marjoram, Sweet	Stems, leaves	Stems, leaves	Leaves
Mint			
Apple (Variegated)	Stems, leaves	Stems, leaves	Leaves
Bergamot	" "	" "	"
English	" "	" "	"
Pepper	" "	" "	"
Spear	" "	" "	"
Mullein	Stems, leaves	Stems, leaves	Stems, leaves
Oregano	Stems, leaves	Stems, leaves	Leaves
Parsley	Stems, leaves	Stems, leaves	Leaves
Pennyroyal	Stems, leaves	Stems, leaves	Leaves
Pyrethrum	Flower heads	Flower heads	Petals
Rose Geranium	Unlikely to be a demand	Leaves	Leaves
Rosemary	Stems, leaves	Stems, leaves	Leaves
Rue	Stems, leaves	Stems, leaves	Leaves
Saffron Crocus	Stigma, styles	Stigma, styles	Stigma, styles
Sage, Broad Leaf	Stems, leaves	Stems, leaves	Leaves
Sage, Narrow Leaf	Stems, leaves	Stems, leaves	Leaves

Herb	Part to Harvest When Selling the Herb Fresh	Part to Harvest for Drying	Part to Package or Process for Selling Dried
Santolina	Stems, leaves	Stems, leaves	Leaves
Savory, Summer	Whole plant	Whole plant	Leaves
Savory, Winter	Stems, leaves	Stems, leaves	Leaves
Shallots	Bulbs	Bulbs	Bulbs
Sorrel	Leaves	Leaves	Leaves
Southernwood	Stems, leaves	Stems, leaves	Leaves
Sweet Cicely	Stems, leaves	Stems, leaves, seeds	Leaves, seeds
Tansy	Stems, leaves	Stems, leaves	Leaves
Tarragon, French	Stems, leaves	Stems, leaves	Leaves
Thyme, Garden	Stems, leaves	Stems, leaves	Leaves
Thyme, Lemon	Stems, leaves	Stems, leaves	Leaves
Thyme, *Serpyllum*	usually sold only as plants		
Thyme, *Barona*	Stems, leaves	Stems, leaves	Leaves
Thyme, Various	usually sold only as plants		
Verbena, Lemon	Soft stems, Leaves	Soft stems, Leaves	Leaves
Woodruff, Sweet	Stems, leaves	Stems, leaves	Soft stems, leaves
Wormwood	Leaves	Leaves	Leaves

WORMWOOD (*Artemisia absinthium*)

Appendix D

Recommended Books
(Mentioned in Text)

New Low-Cost Sources of Energy for the Home, by Peter Clegg. Garden Way Publishing, Charlotte, VT 05445. $5.95 (pbk), $8.95 (case)

Let It Rot! The Home Gardening Guide to Composting, by Stu Campbell. Garden Way Publishing, Charlotte, VT 05445. $3.95 (pbk)

The Bug Book: Harmless Insect Controls, by Helen and John Philbrick. Garden Way Publishing, Charlotte, VT 05445. $3.95 (pbk)

Comfrey Report: The Story of the World's Fastest Protein Builder, by Lawrence D. Hills. North Central Comfrey Products, Box 195, Glidden, WI 54527. $4.50

Handbook on Propagation. Brooklyn Botanic Garden, 100 Washington Avenue, Brooklyn, NY 11225 (1957). $1.50 (paper)

Growing Herbs for the Kitchen, by Betty E. M. Jacobs. Gray's Publishing, Ltd. P.O. Box 2160, Sidney, British Columbia, Canada V8L 3S6 (1972). $5.95

Plant Propagation in Pictures, by Montague Free. American Garden Guild, Inc. and Doubleday & Co., Inc., Garden City, NY (1957). Obtainable from Garden Way Publishing. $7.95 (case)

Potpourri, Incense, and Other Fragrant Concoctions, by Ann Tucker. Workman Publishing Company, 231 East 51 St., New York, NY 10022 (1972). $2.45 (spiral pbk)

Fragrance: How to Make Natural Soaps, Scents and Sundries, by Beverley Plummer. Atheneum Publishers, 122 East 42 Street, New York, NY 10017 (1975). $8.95 (case)

Herbs, Health and Cookery, by Phillipa Back and Claire Lowenfield. Universal Publishing and Distributing Corp., Award Books, 350 Kennedy Drive, Hauppage, NY 11788 (1970). $1.25

Appendix E

Herb Growers & Suppliers

This appendix lists names of growers and suppliers of Herb seeds and/or plants.

I would like to take the opportunity of thanking all of them for answering my questions, especially those who also sent their catalogs, enabling me to list fuller information about their operations.

(If you sell Herb plants and seeds and are not listed here, or if you *are* listed here, and any details are not correct, please write to me care of Garden Way Publishing, so that additions and alterations may be made in the next edition of *Profitable Herb-Growing at Home*. Please send a copy of current catalog with your letter.)

United States

CALIFORNIA

California Herb Growers. P.O. Box 925 (Quarry Road) San Marcos, CA 92069. They have no catalog. They sell Herb plants both at the farm and by mail order. They say "No retail inquiries answered—mainly wholesale to brokers." They would seem to be large scale suppliers.

J. L. Hudson, Seedsman—A World Seed Service. P.O. Box 1058, Redwood City, CA 94064. Send 50 cents for their catalog. They sell Herb seeds wholesale and retail.

Excellent listing of commonplace and hard to find varieties. Latin and common names given.

Redwood City Seed Co. (Craig Dremann) P.O. Box 361, Redwood City, CA 94064. Send 25 cents for their catalog. They sell Herb seeds both retail and wholesale by mail order only. They will ship Comfrey and Aloe vera plants; also Ginseng and Golden Seal in season. They say "we print a quarterly list of rare and unusual seeds of which we can only secure small quantities—such as Valerian and Lobelia inflata." An unusual and interesting listing. Latin and common names given.

Clyde Robin Seed Co. Inc. P.O. Box 2855, Castro Valley, CA 94546. Telephone (415) 581-3467. Send $1 for their catalog. They sell Herb seeds wholesale and retail.

Taylors Herb Garden, Inc. 1535 Lone Oak Road, Vista, CA 92083. Telephone (714) 727-3485. Send 25 cents for their catalog. They sell Herb plants both retail and wholesale, at the gardens and by mail order, shipping by UPS, by truck and by air. They say "Conducted tours every two months over two acres of labeled Herbs both cultivated and wild."

CONNECTICUT

Capriland's Herb Farm (Adelma Grenier Simmons). Silver Street, Coventry, CT 06238. Telephone (203) 742-7244. Catalog free. Open daily 9 A.M. to 5 P.M. April through December. She sells Herb seeds and Herb plants at the farm and by mail order; shipping by UPS.

Comstock, Ferre & Co. 263 Main Street, Wethersfield, CT 06109. Telephone (203)

529-3319. Their catalog is free. Open daily
9 A.M. to 3 P.M. They sell Herb seeds. They
do not ship Herb plants, but sell them at
the above address. Good listing of common Herbs; Latin and common names
given.

The Chas. C. Hart Seed Co. Main and Hart
Street, Wethersfield, CT 06109. Telephone (203) 529-2537. Their catalog is
free. Open Monday to Saturday 9:30 A.M.
to 6:00 P.M. Sundays 1 P.M. to 6 P.M. They
sell Herb seeds wholesale and retail.

Hemlock Hill Herb Farm (Mrs. Dorothy
Childs Hogner). Hemlock Hill Road,
Litchfield, CT 06759. Telephone (203)
567-5031. Send 50 cents for catalog. Open
to visitors Tuesday to Saturday 10 A.M. to
4 P.M. May 1 to August 31, or by appointment. She sells Herb plants at the farm
and by mail order, but wholesale only at
the farm. She ships them by parcel post,
special handling. Good listing of perennial Herb plants. Latin and common
names given.

Herb Shop. (P.O. Box 362), 15 Sherman
Street, Fairfield, CT 06430. Telephone
(203) 255-4004. Send 50 cents for catalog.
They sell Herb seeds. They do not ship
Herb plants, but sell them at the above
address. Only a small Herb seed listing,
but they carry many Herb products.

Logee's Greenhouses. 55 North Street,
Danielson, CT 06239. Send $1.50 for
catalog. Open to visitors daily 9 A.M. to 5
P.M. They sell Herb plants at the above
address and by mail order (retail only);
shipping by UPS, air mail and fourth class
parcel post. Minimum order $10.

Sunny Border Nurseries, Inc. 1709 Kensington Road, Kensington, CT 06037. Telephone (203) 828-5771. Their catalog is free. They sell Herb plants by mail order and at the farm. *Wholesale only.* They ship by UPS, air freight and by bus. They say, "We specialize in perennial Herbs which are propagated from top cuttings."

FLORIDA

The Yarb Patch. 3726 Thomasville Road, Tallahassee, FL 32303. Send 25 cents for their catalog. They sell Herb seeds and plants both at the Patch and by mail order. Plants are shipped by UPS April through June and in October and November.

If you wish to buy at wholesale give them 60 days notice. They have a good listing of many culinary varieties of Herb seeds and plants. Latin and common names are given. They also offer some Scented Geraniums.

They say, "The Patch and Shop are open from 10 A.M. to 5 P.M. Monday through Saturday, except for June through August when our summer hours will be noon to 5 P.M., Monday through Friday, and 10 A.M. to 5 P.M. Saturdays. Closed all Sundays." They also sell Herb products.

MAINE

Howe Hill Herbs. Camden, ME 04843. Telephone (207) 763-3506. Send 35 cents for catalog. Open to visitors June through September. They sell Herb plants by mail order, shipping by UPS and parcel post. They also sell seeds of annual Herbs.

Good listing of common and uncommon Herbs. Specialists in scented leaved, Miniature and Dwarf Geraniums.

Johnny's Selected Seeds. Albion, ME 04910. Telephone (207) 437-4303. Send 50 cents for catalog. They sell Herb seeds, both common and not so common, and medicinal.

Thomas Seeds (Carl Thomas). Winthrop, ME 04364. Telephone (207) 377-6724. Their catalog is free. They sell Herb seeds by mail and Herb plants at the above address, both wholesale and retail.

They say that their catalog is rather unique" . . . designed with the northern vegetable grower in mind, seeds of varieties proven in the cold climate of Maine."

Carroll Gardens. (P.O. Box 310), 444 East Main Street, Westminster, MD 21157. Telephone (301) 848-5422. Catalog free. Visitors always welcomed. They sell Herb plants at the gardens and by mail order; shipping by UPS. Good list, with many uncommon varieties. Discounts on Herbs to clubs on plant sales.

MARYLAND

The Herbiary and Potpourri Shop. Childs Homestead Road, Orleans, MA 02653. Telephone (617) 255-4422. No catalog. Open Monday to Friday, 9 A.M. to 5 P.M. They sell Herb seeds and plants at the above address, where they have Herb Gardens open to visitors.

MASSACHUSETTS

Dutch Mountain Nursery. 7984 North 48th Street, R. 1, Augusta, MI 49012. Send 25 cents for catalog. They sell Herb plants by mail order only, shipping plants in 2¼-inch pots.

MICHIGAN

Fox Hill Farm. (P.O. Box 7), 434 Michigan Avenue, Parma, MI 49269. Send 50 cents for catalog. Open to visitors Thursdays and Sundays only, noon to 6 P.M. They sell Herb plants at the farm and by mail order;

shipping by UPS. Their catalog is exceptionally well presented with many common and hard-to-find Herbs. Latin and common names given. They also list a good selection of Scented Geraniums.

MISSOURI

A.B.C. Herb Nursery and Greenhouses. R. 1, Box 313, Lecoma, MO 65540. Telephone (314) 435-6389. Send 25 cents for their catalog. They sell Herb plants (retail only) at the farm and by mail order, shipping by parcel post.

NEW JERSEY

Mincemoyer Nursery. W. County Line Road, Jackson, NJ 08527. Telephone (201) 363-3215. Send 25 cents for catalog. They sell Herb plants at the farm and by mail order.

Rocky Hollow Herb Farm. Box 707, Sussex, NJ 07461. Telephone (201) 875-5132. Send 25 cents for their catalog. They sell Herb seeds both wholesale and retail.

Thompson and Morgan, Inc. 403 Kennedy Blvd., Somerdale, NJ 08083. Telephone (609) 784-8600. Their catalog is free. They sell Herb seeds by mail order both wholesale and retail. This is the U.S. address of this well-known British Seedhouse. Their listing is comprehensive, and Latin and common names are given.

Well-Sweep Herb Farm (Cyrus and Louise Hyde). 317 Mt. Bethel Road, Port Murray, NJ 07865. Telephone (201) 853-5390. Catalog free. Display Herb garden open to visitors Monday to Saturday 9:30 A.M. to 5 P.M. Sunday by appointment only. They sell Herb seeds and Herb plants at the farm and by mail order; shipping by

UPS and parcel post. Excellent listing of common and uncommon Herbs, and Scented Geraniums.

Herbst Bros., Seedsmen, Inc. 1000 Main Street, Brewster, NY 10509. Telephone (914) 379-2971. Their catalog is free. They sell Herb seeds both retail and wholesale, but have a $25 minimum order on new accounts to commercial growers. They have a good listing of the more common Herbs under their Latin and common names.

Joseph Harris Company, Inc. Moreton Farm, Rochester, NY 14624. Telephone (716) 594-9411. They sell Herb seeds. They do not ship Herb plants, but sell them at the above address.

Martin Viette Nurseries. Rt. 25A, East Norwich, NY 11732. Telephone (516) 922-5530. Send $1.50 for catalog. They sell Herb plants wholesale and retail at the farm.

Garden Place. 6780 Heisley Road, Mentor, OH 44060. Telephone (216)255-3705. Send 50 cents for their catalog. They sell plants wholesale and retail at the farm and by mail order. The plants are shipped bare root, packed with spaghnum moss on roots and layers of excelsior. They are specialists in field grown perennial plants including Herbs.

Glecklers Seedmen. Metamora, OH 43540. Catalog free. They sell Herb seeds.

McComb Greenhouse. Rt. 1, New Straits-ville, OH 43766. Telephone (614) 394-2239. Send 35 cents for their catalog. They sell Herb plants (retail only) both at the greenhouse and by mail order, shipping via UPS, air mail or however specified on order. They say, "We welcome visitors to our greenhouse, open seven days a week from 9 A.M. to 5 P.M. Many different and unusual plants from all over the world." They have a short but unusual Herb list, in which both Latin and common names are given.

Mellinger's Inc. North Lima, OH 44452. Telephone (216) 549-9861. Catalog free. Open Monday to Saturday, 8 A.M. to 5 P.M. They sell Herb seeds and Herb plants at the farm, and by mail order.

Ohio Comfrey Growers, Inc. Route 1, Box 289A, Millersport, OH 43047. Free price list. They sell Comfrey roots at the above address and by mail order; shipping by UPS, bus and parcel post. Minimum order 20 roots.

Sunnybrook Farms Nursery. 9448 Mayfield Road, Chesterland, OH 44026. Telephone (216) 729-7232. Send 50 cents for catalog. Open Tuesday to Saturday, 9 A.M. to 5:30 P.M. They sell Herb plants at the farm and by mail order; shipping by UPS and parcel post. They list culinary, medicinal and fragrant Herbs.

OREGON

Herbs 'n Honey Nursery (Mrs. Chester C. Fisher, Jr.). Route 2, Box 205, Monmouth, OR 97361. Telephone (503) 623-4033. Send 25 cents for catalog. Open year 'round Monday through Friday, 8 A.M. to 4 P.M. Weekends by appointment. She sells Herb seeds and plants at the farm and by mail order, both wholesale and retail.

Good listing of perennial Herb plants, including many Alliums, Artemisias,

Lavenders, Mints and Sages, also Scented Geraniums. Latin and common names given.

Nichols Garden Nursery. 1190 North Pacific Highway, Albany, OR 97321. Telephone (503) 928-9280. Catalog free. Open Monday to Saturday, 9 A.M. to 5:30 P.M. They sell Herb seeds and Herb plants at the farm, and by mail order; shipping by UPS and air mail.

W. Atlee Burpee Co. Warminster, PA 18974. Telephone (215) 674-4900. Catalog free. They sell Herb seeds and Herb plants by mail order; shipping by UPS and special handling parcel post. They also sell Shallots and Garlic.

PENNSYLVANIA

Metro Myster Farms. Route 1, Box 285, Northampton, PA 18067. Telephone (215) 262-6205. Send 25 cents for catalog. They sell Herb seeds and plants at the farm and by mail order; shipping by UPS and special handling parcel post. They also sell Shallots, Elephant Garlic, Comfrey and Jerusalem Artichokes.

Greene Herb Gardens Inc. Greene, RI 02827. Telephone (401) 397-3652. Send stamped self-addressed envelope for seed list which includes both common and hard to find varieties of Herb seeds; they sell by mail order, retail only.

RHODE ISLAND

Meadowbrook Herb Garden. Wyoming, RI 02898. Telephone (401) 539-7603. Send 50 cents for catalog. Open Monday to Saturday, 10 A.M. to 12 noon, and 1 P.M. to 5 P.M., Sundays 1 P.M. to 4 P.M. They sell Herb seeds. They do not ship Herb plants, but sell them at the above address.

SOUTH CAROLINA

George W. Park Seed Co., Inc. Greenwood, SC 29647. Telephone (803) 374-3341. Catalog free. Open Monday to Friday 8 A.M. to 4:30 P.M. They sell Herb seeds and plants by mail, and at the above address. They ship by UPS and parcel post.

TEXAS

Hilltop Herb Farm. P.O. Box 866, Cleveland TX 77327. Telephone (714) 592-5859. Send $1 for catalog, or 35 cents for list. Open year 'round. Store and greenhouse hours, Friday and Saturday 10 A.M. to 4 P.M., Sundays 2 P.M. to 4 P.M. Closed Mondays and holidays. They sell Herb seeds and plants by mail order and at the farm, retail only. Plants shipped October through April only by UPS and bus.

Yankee Peddler Herb Farm. Route 4, Box 76, Hwy. 36 N, Brenham, TX 77833. Telephone (713) 836-4442. Send $1 for a clear and comprehensive catalog, or 25 cents for list. Open to visitors daily 9 A.M. to 5 P.M. except on major holidays. They sell Herb seeds and plants at the farm and by mail order, retail and wholesale. They ship air mail or bus as customers wish. Excellent listing of commonplace and hard to find varieties. Latin and common names given in catalog.

VERMONT

Le Jardin du Gourmet (Raymond Saufroy). West Danville, VT 05873. Telephone (802) 684-2201. Send 25 cents for catalog. He sells Herb seeds and plants by mail order, and at the farm after May 15th; shipping by UPS and parcel post. He says, "We're the people who first sold shallots to the U.S. public in 1958—we also sell leek transplants." He imports stock from France.

Cedarbrook Herb Farm (Don and Karman McReynolds). Route 5, Box 1258, Sequim, WA 98382. Telephone (206) 683-4541. Send 25 cents for catalog. Open April through September, Monday to Saturday, 10 A.M. to 4 P.M. Closed Sundays and holidays. They sell Herb plants at the farm. Good listing of common and hard to find Herbs. They also sell Scented Geraniums, Shallots and Elephant Garlic.

WASHINGTON

Lamb Nurseries. 101 E. Sharp Avenue, Spokane, WA 99202. Telephone (508) 328-7956. Their catalog is free. They sell Herb plants wholesale and retail at the nurseries and by mail order; shipping by UPS, parcel post or air parcel post.

The Herb Cottage. Washington Cathedral, Mount St. Alban, Washington, D.C., 20016. Catalog free. They sell Herb seeds by mail order and Herb products.

WASHINGTON, D.C.

Hickory Hollow. Route 1, Box 52, Peterstown, WV 24963. Telephone (304) 753-9817. Send 25 cents for catalog. They sell Herb seeds by mail order, and Herb products.

WEST VIRGINIA

North Central Comfrey Products. Box 195, Glidden, WI 54527. Telephone (715) 264-2083. Catalog free. They sell Comfrey planting stock, root cuttings, crowns and plants at the farm and by mail order, shipping by parcel post.

WISCONSIN

Canada

ONTARIO

Ashby's Garden Centre and Nursery. R.R. 2, Cameron, Ontario K0M 1G0. Telephone (705) 359-1115. Send 30 cents for catalog. Open for Herb plant sales Thursday through Saturday. They also sell Herb seeds and plants by mail order. Catalog gives full details. Retail and wholesale sales. Excellent listing of common and many hard to find varieties. Latin and common names given. They also sell Shallots, Elephant Garlic and Garlic, and many other Alliums and Comfrey.

Otto Richter and Sons Ltd. P.O. Box 26-G, Goodwood, Ontario L0C 1A0. Telephone (416) 294-1457. Send 50 cents for catalog. Open from 9 A.M. to 5 P.M. seven days a week. Open most days of the year. However, please phone to be certain.
   They sell Herb seeds by mail order, and Herb seeds and plants at the farm (Canadian customers enquire re shipping plants). Excellent listing, including many unusual and rare Herb seeds. Latin and common names given.

Stokes Seeds, Ltd. 39 James Street, St. Catharines, Ontario. Telephone (416) 685-4255. Catalog free. They sell Herb seeds by mail and at their store.

PRINCE EDWARD
ISLAND

Rosmarinus Herbs (Linda Gilkeson). R.R.1, Souris, PEI, C0A 2B0. Telephone (902) 687-3460. Her catalog is free. She sells wholesale and retail Herb seeds and plants at the farm. She sells perennial Herb plants by mail order in the Maritime provinces of Canada. The Herb plants are organically grown.

She has an interesting and comprehensive listing. Latin and common names are given.

The Village Pottery (W. James Murray). Mill Village, Queens County, NS. Telephone (902) 677-2776. He specializes in Comfrey. Selling cuttings and small plants at the farm and by mail order, shipping by parcel post. Inquire about other Herb plants.

NOVA SCOTIA

PENNYROYAL (*Mentha pulegium*)

220

Index

A

Agrimonia eupatoria, see Agrimony
Agrimony, *illus. 118,* 137
Air fresheners, 108, 175
Alkanet, *illus. 83,* 137
Alkanna tinctoria, see Alkanet
Allium ascalonicum, see Shallots
Allium sativum, see Garlic
Allium schoenoprasum, see Chives
Allium tuberosum, see Garlic chives
American Pennyroyal, *see* Pennyroyal
Anethum graveolens, see Dill
Angelica, *illus. xii,* 2, 34, 36; candied, 164–65
Angelica archangelica, see Angelica
Anise, *illus. 11,* 40, 42, 117; candy, 167
Annuals, harvesting, 81
Anthemis nobilis, see Chamomile, English, or Roman
Anthriscum cerefolium, see Chervil
Apple Mint (Variegated), *see* Mint
Artemesia abrotanum, see Southernwood
Artemesia absinthium, see Wormwood
Artemesia dracunculus, see French Tarragon
Asperula odorata, see Sweet Woodruff

B

Baked goods, Herb-flavored, 170
Balm Lemon, *see* Lemon Balm
Basil, Bush, *illus. 124,* 138
Basil, Sweet, *illus. 17,* 42; for profit, 92; seeds, 56; vinegar, 161
Bath perfume, 175
Bay, 2–3, 138, *illus. 139*
Beds, layout of, 5, 9-10; for Chives, 121–22, 123, 125; for Parsley, 114, 116
Bedstraw, *illus. 117,* 138
Bee garden, Herbs for, 48 (list), 157 (list)

Bergamot, *illus. 140,* 141
Bergamot (or Orange) Mint, *see* Mint
Borage, *illus. 4, 42;* candied, 165
Borago officinalis, see Borage
Bouquet Garni, 3, 169–70
Builder's sand, 18
Bulbs, 63 (list), 78
Burnet, Salad, *illus. 132,* 141; vinegar, 161
Bush Basil, *see* Basil, Bush

C

Calendula, *illus. 134,* 141
Calendula officinalis, see Calendula or Pot Marigold
Candied Herbs, 95 (list); how to make, 164–65, 167
Candy, Herb-flavored, 95 (list); how to make, 167
Caraway, *illus. 22,* 40; for profit, 92.
Carum carvi, see Caraway
Carum petroselium, see Parsley
Catnip, 38, *illus. 39,* 108; toys, 2, 177–78
Chamomile, English or Roman, *illus. 127,* 141
Chamomile, German, 142, *illus. 196*
Chervil, 42, *illus. 43;* for Christmas sales, 102; for profit, 92
Cheshunt compound fungicide, 56
Chive plants, selling of, 131, 133
Chives, 1, 13, 28, 30, 84, *illus. 120,* 121–33; beds, 121–22, 123, 125; for Christmas sales, 104; for profit, 93, 129–33; harvesting, 126, 128; packaging, 128; replanting, 125; seeds, 54, 122–23
Chives, Garlic, *see* Garlic Chives
Chrysanthemum cinerariaefolium, see Pyrethrum

221

Sweet Cicely, 3, 38, *illus. 103;* candied, 165
Sweet Marjoram, *see* Marjoram
Sweet Woodruff, *see* Woodruff
Symphytum peregrinum, see Comfrey

T

Tanacetum vulgare, see Tansy
Tansy, 150, *illus. 151*
Tarragon, French, 1, 26, 28, *illus. 107;* for Christmas sales, 104–5; for profit, 93; propagation of, 64; vinegar, 161
Tarragon, Russian, 26
Tea, Herbs for, 49 (list), 157 (list), 168–69; labelling, 169; packaging, 169; processing, 87
Thyme, 34, 150, 153; for Christmas sales, 105; jelly, 164; vinegar, 161; wreaths, 172
Thyme, English (or Winter), 34
Thyme, French (or Summer), 34
Thyme, Garden, 3, 34, *illus. 115;* for Christmas sales, 105; jelly, 164
Thyme, Lemon, 28, *illus. 29;* for Christmas sales, 105; propagation of, 64
Thymus citrodorus, see Thyme, Lemon

Thymus doerfleri, see Thyme
Thymus erectus, see Thyme
Thymus herba-barona, see Thyme
Thymus serpyllum, see Thyme
Thymes, Various (*Thymus species*), *illus. 192*
Thymus vulgaris, see Thyme, Garden
Tools, 5–6
Transplanting, 14, 50–51, 58
Transplanting shock, 14
Tussie Mussies, 96, 172; outlets, 172

V

Variegated Apple Mint, *see* Mint
Verbascum thapsus, see Mullein
Verbena, Lemon, 2–3, *illus. 152, 153;* jelly, 164
Vinegar, 95 (list); how to make 159–61

W

Watering, 51, 52, 54–55, 58
Windmill, 20
Winter Savory, *see* Savory
Woodruff, Sweet, 3, 84, 153, *illus. 200*
Wormwood, 154
Wreaths, 96, 172; outlets for, 172